Freeze With Ease

Freeze
With Ease

MARIAN FOX BURROS

AND

LOIS LEVINE

The Macmillan Company, New York
Collier-Macmillan Limited, London

ILLUSTRATED BY ROSALIE PETRASH

ACKNOWLEDGMENTS

Our book is dedicated not only to our long-suffering husbands and neglected families but also to some very special friends who gave great assistance, counsel and sympathy: Sherley Koteen, whose always gentle but precise criticism made the book a great deal more readable; Helen Fox, who willingly proofread the entire manuscript; Mary Lacy, who has encouraged and suggested from the very beginning; and Emanuel Linhardt, without whose help this book would never have been in print.

MARIAN FOX BURROS
LOIS LEVINE

Contents

INTRODUCTION

Since everyone takes polls these days to find out what the man in the street thinks about politics or what the consumer wants to purchase, we decided to take our own private poll of the woman in the kitchen to find out what sort of cookbook she wants. It wasn't exactly a scientific random sampling à la Mr. Gallup, but we did quiz all our friends and anyone we happened to meet at the checkout counter of the neighborhood supermarket and they all said the same thing: a book on home freezing *with good recipes.*

One friend, the mother of six, called this summer to say she was having a family of eight (including six children) come to visit for five days, and what could she put into her freezer in advance? After thinking what we would do in such a case—preferably put ourselves in the deep freeze until they left—we sat down with her and were able to plan menus for the "duration" that enabled our friend to enjoy her company.

Home freezers, whether freestanding or in combination with a refrigerator, have revolutionized home cooking. They have banished leftovers and the usual cry of "What, that again?" because meal remnants now may be frozen to reappear weeks later in entirely different guise. Meals, therefore, can have a wider variety within any given week without sacrificing economy. Even the holiday bird need see service only a day or two before the leftover meat is packaged and frozen. One of the best recommendations for a recipe these days is that it can be made ahead and frozen. With the right assortment of foods in your freezer there is never a need for a last-minute flurry at mealtime, either for family or company meals. And for those of us busy modern women who sometimes arrive home at dinnertime, it's a real comfort to dive into the freezer for an already cooked meal that needs only to be reheated. While the meal is warming you can set the table, toss the salad and even manage a peek at the evening newspaper.

Day in and day out, a freezer is a dependable, steady performer, and, like all good performers, it has certain moments of brilliance. When unexpected guests arrive at mealtime, it is no longer necessary to push the panic button. Cooked foods can magically appear, having been prepared many weeks before by the gal who was foresighted enough to "make one for the table and one for the freezer."

To help you make your freezer work for you and turn it into more than just a repository for lamb chops and TV dinners, we set to work searching for ideas and recipes that would "freeze with ease." There are many claims about what can and cannot be frozen and what does and does not taste good after freezing. If there is one conclusion that we have come to after years of tasting and testing it is "Don't take anyone's word for it—try it yourself!" This includes recipes from dietitians, home economists, gourmets, other cookbooks, magazines and newspapers, as well as those from next-door neighbors and Aunt Minnies. We are even wary of recipes concocted in such and such a test kitchen, since none of our cookbook users can duplicate such ideal conditions. Certainly we can't! Our recipes have been tested in our own kitchens, which are like those in any other homes where doors slam and children cry. Then they are eaten by our testers—our families and friends with tastes ranging from the ordinary to the gourmet—at anything from family lunch to an elegant dinner party.

In addition every recipe in this book has been tested for post-defrosting appeal. Perhaps we have unusually demanding standards on taste and appearance, but we just don't like the way certain foods look or taste after defrosting. They won't poison you, but we doubt if they will whet your appetite either. So these foods are not recommended in our book, but you'll be delightfully surprised to see the number of freezables we have found.

On the other hand, much has been written about cream sauces separating and fried foods turning rancid and tough. In a period of two months or more none of these things has taken place in our freezers, and we promise that if you follow our cooking, wrapping and serving directions you will have the same good luck.

Almost every recipe included is fairly simple to prepare, but we could not resist a few that take a bit of extra preparation time and an exotic ingredient or two. We consider them so absolutely sure-fire to make you the talk of the town that they are more than worth the effort involved. Since each can be prepared in stages—whenever you have a half hour or so—and each stage frozen, the *final* putting together takes very little time.

Although we have tried to cover all aspects of freezer use, we have said nothing about commercial freezer plans or the purchase of whole sides of beef. In the case of the former, we much prefer to select our own food, but if you are a person who can never get to the store conveniently and you are absolutely positive that the plan costs you no more than store buying—go ahead.

As far as sides of beef go, you must be sure, of course, that your source meets all health standards, that you are really saving money, that you can use each cut of meat you get and that you don't need the storage space for other freezables. Above all, you must own a very large freezer!

A note or two in the use of this book may be helpful here.

Shallots are often called for in the recipes. They are a member of the onion family, the size of a large clove of garlic. Shallots are available in many specialty grocery stores and some supermarkets. Since they keep for long periods of time, buy a pound when you find them and store in a cool, dry place.

If it is impossible to find shallots, substitute green onions (scallions).

Instant blending flour. In many instances this flour can be used interchangeably with regular flour, although additional liquid may be required in some cases.

The first section of the book deals with all technical matters relating to freezers and frozen foods. The next three sections are filled with recipes and menus suitable for every conceivable type of meal. And so to freeze with ease . . .

1

Cold Hands, Warm Heart

Cold Hands, Warm Heart

BASIC RULES FOR USING THE FREEZER

VARIETY OF FREEZERS AVAILABLE

If you do not already own a freezer, there are a variety of models now available to start you joyously on the road to freezer living.

Separate home freezers come in two styles: chest and upright. The chest offers the useful feature of the top as a work surface if the freezer is in the kitchen or pantry; but it takes up more space than the upright and as a result usually goes to the basement. Also, it often requires much bending and fumbling to find the item you want—inevitably the one at the bottom. (Mittens are very handy in this case, and a pair should be hung beside the chest freezer.)

The upright freezer is somewhat more convenient to use and organize. If you plan to install it in your kitchen or pantry (much to be desired, says one who runs to the basement freezer several times a day) remember the upright requires much less floor space than the chest. Searching for packages is kept to a minimum, and if your freezer is manually defrosted, an upright is easier to defrost than a chest. In the newer uprights with removable and adjustable shelves and storage baskets, the bulky irregularly shaped packages present no problem—a drawback in the older models.

If you cannot accommodate a separate freezer, you can still enjoy zero-degree freezer space in your home. The two-door combination refrigerator-freezer, today's most popular model, offers the convenience of fresh food storage along with a separately insulated and refrigerated freezer in the same cabinet. Refrigerator-freezers have a separate door for the freezer section: the freezer may be located at

3

the top, at the bottom, or at the side. Take your choice, but whatever you do, be sure to insist on a big, big freezer section.

In uprights and two-door combination refrigerator-freezers, you can choose either an automatic defrosting type or nonautomatic (manual). The automatics feature forced-air circulation and provide for uniform cold distribution throughout the freezer. In the upright models, the automatics usually have a quick-freezing compartment as opposed to the fast-freezing shelves in the nonautomatics. Of course the primary benefit of the automatic is to relieve you of the time and annoyance involved in defrosting. Automatics also have two other benefits since frost never forms: 1) packages stay clear, easy to read and handle; 2) ice and frost can't collect on freezer walls to take up space, lessen refrigerating efficiency and increase cost of operation.

What type is best for you? The decision is yours. Obviously, if you prefer a two-door refrigerator-freezer model, the size of the freezer is limited. Whatever you do, buy the largest freezer section available in the style you select. If it's a separate freezer (upright or chest), be sure you get one that's big enough. Allow a minimum of 3 to 4 cubic feet per person for a separate freezer. A freezer has a long life and it would be a shame to spend all those years regretting that you didn't buy the right size. Remember our final word of advice: "Buy it bigger than you originally planned."

DEFROSTING THE FREEZER

The basic rules for the operation of your freezer will come in a booklet put out by the manufacturer, which should be consulted for general information. If your freezer does not have automatic defrosting, we recommend that you defrost whenever an accumulation of frost—a half-inch or more—gathers on the surface. Frost cuts down on your freezer's efficiency and increases the cost of operation. If the freezer is in a relatively warm place and is opened frequently, it will require more frequent defrosting than if it is placed in a cool spot and seldom opened. When you contemplate a thorough defrosting job, let your freezer stock dwindle so there won't be too much to keep frozen while the appliance is unplugged. To get the food as cold as possible before defrosting, set the control at the lowest setting for a few hours. Wrap the frozen food in newspapers or towels and stack closely in boxes to keep cold. Gently scrape the frost with a dull instrument to facilitate its removal. To speed defrosting set pans of hot water on a few shelves. After the defrosting is complete, wash the inside surfaces with warm water and baking soda, dry thoroughly, close the door, and set the control at coldest for ten minutes before returning the foods.

This time and inconvenience can of course be eliminated if you own an automatic defrosting model.

IF THE POWER FAILS

Since a freezer owner usually has a great deal of money in "frozen assets," it is handy to know how to protect this investment in case of power failure! Before panic sets in, check the plug and fuse. Then call the repairman. Next step is to keep the freezer door closed. Do not peek, which will permit precious cold air to escape. If your freezer is fully stocked the contents will remain frozen for at least two days; if half-full, at least one full day.

If the power remains off for a longer time, buy dry ice at the rate of 25 pounds for each 10 cubic feet of freezer, and place it (with gloved hands), in the largest chunks possible, on top of the foods. In a fully loaded freezer this will be effective for 3 to 4 days; in a half-loaded one, 2 to 3 days.

Two further alternatives would be to rent space in a commercial locker or to beg space from a friend or friends.

If thawing should take place all is not lost. All uncooked foods, of course, may be cooked and frozen again. Baked goods may safely be refrozen after thawing but they may be somewhat dried out.

According to the House and Garden Bulletin #69, issued by the Department of Agriculture, "If foods have thawed only partially and there are still ice crystals in the package, they may be safely refrozen." Even this partial thawing reduces quality, of course. A frozen item is "thawed only partially" when the temperature of the package does not rise above 40°. If in doubt, place a thermometer between the wrappings and the food. It is also suggested that the refrozen foods be used in advance of other frozen foods.

REFREEZING—WHY NOT?
QUICK FREEZING

There are many chemical statistics, which we will not go into, that explain why freezing of completely thawed foods is unwise. At any rate, it is the unanimous opinion of all food chemists that it is only courting danger to refreeze completely thawed foods (with the exception of baked goods).

Quick freezing is recommended because it preserves the food in a condition nearest to the one in which it was when fresh. This all has to do with enzymes and such, but just take our word for it! Place the items to be frozen directly in contact with your fast freeze shelves, not on top of other packages, and allow air to circulate around the packages. Do not freeze too much food at one time, thus raising the temperature in your freezer. A good rule of thumb is to freeze up to one-tenth of the total amount your freezer holds. If it holds 600 pounds, freeze up to 60 pounds at a time.

LENGTH OF STORAGE TIME*

If the chart seems to allow for much latitude it is only because there does not seem to be more than very general agreement on how long various foods may be stored without loss of flavor or quality. Our experience has been that the longer time is more accurate. Just remember that almost nothing improves while sitting in the freezer. On the other hand, wholesomeness (safety) is not involved in overlong freezing—the taste may change but not the safety in eating.

* At 0°. This is very important, because foods may not be stored as long at higher temperatures.

FOOD	MAXIMUM STORAGE TIME IN MONTHS
Beef	
Roasts and steaks	12 to 14
Ground beef	8
Lamb	
Roasts and chops	12
Pork *	
Roasts and chops	8 to 12
Sausage, seasoned	2 to 4
Sausage, unseasoned	6 to 8
Bacon	2 to 4
Ham	2 to 4
Veal	
Cutlets and chops	6 to 8
Roasts	8 to 10
Variety meats	
Kidneys, brains, etc.	4 to 6
Poultry	
Chicken, turkey	8 to 12
Duck, goose and game	6
Chicken livers	3
Fish	
Shellfish	up to 10
Fatty fish	6 to 8
Lean fish	8 to 12
Fruits	
Citrus fruits and juices	4 to 6
Other fruits	8 to 12
Vegetables †	10 to 12
Dairy products	
Butter, salted	1 to 3
Butter, unsalted	6
Cheese, hard	up to 6
Cream and cottage cheese	up to 4
Cream	2 to 4
Milk ‡	½ to 1
Eggs	up to 12
Ice cream	1 to 2

* Three weeks or more at 0° kills any trichinosis organism that might be present in pork.

† Onions—up to 3 months, unblanched.

‡ For emergency use only.

FOOD	MAXIMUM STORAGE TIME IN MONTHS
Baked goods	
Breads, rolls, cakes	12
Sponge and angel cakes	6
Cookies	6 to 12
Pies *	6 to 8
Pie shells	3
Waffles and pancakes	6
Unbaked goods	
Cake batter	½
Cookie dough	3
Pie shells	3
Pies	4
Yeast breads and rolls	1½
Cooked meat	1
Cooked poultry	1
Combination dishes with meat	4
Combination dishes with poultry	6
Sandwiches	½ to ¾
Canapés and appetizers	1
Soups	4
Steamed puddings	4
Candies	up to 12
Nuts	12

TO THAW OR NOT TO THAW

We would like to state quite flatly that, as long as time permits, we prefer to thaw most foods before cooking (vegetables and unbaked pies are exceptions). The results seem to be more satisfactory. You do not run the risk of hot outsides and cold centers, for even if you are very careful to bake, broil or roast frozen foods very slowly, this may still happen. We also feel that thick cuts of meat retain their juices if thawed before cooking.

Poultry must be at least pliable before it can be cooked.

Cooked meats and poultry should be thawed before being added to another dish and stew should be defrosted at room temperature before other vegetables are added.

* Baked chiffon pies only one month: must include egg whites or whipping cream in the recipe.

Cooking on top of the stove does not present the same problems that oven cooking does. Careful watching or the use of a double boiler will bring satisfactory results when the dish is heated in its frozen state. Soup can be heated and thawed at the same time, as can spaghetti and barbecue sauces.

Remember that a great deal of extra cooking time is required for still-frozen foods. Large frozen roasts may take as much as one and one-half times as long to cook.

Thawing frozen foods in their original wrappings in the refrigerator results in the most uniform thawing and the best appearance of the food, but it takes two to three times longer to defrost in the refrigerator than at room temperature and twice as long as under running water. (Except in a pinch, this latter method is not recommended, however.) If you are in a big hurry an electric fan directly in front of the frozen package gives almost magic results. A small amount of moisture collects on the inside of all frozen packages and containers and if this condensation will ruin the texture of the food, unwrap or remove the cover from the package and cover loosely with fresh paper. The one exception to defrosting in wrappings is baked goods. To prevent them from drying out cover them with fresh paper.

Here are two timetables, one for cooking from the frozen state and one for defrosting frozen foods.

Cooking Frozen Foods

FOOD	METHOD	TIME
Beef		
Rib	Roast at 300°	38 to 45 minutes per pound rare
		42 to 50 minutes per pound medium
		47 to 65 minutes per pound well
Rolled	Roast at 300°	48 to 55 minutes per pound rare
		52 to 60 minutes per pound medium
		55 to 70 minutes per pound well
Round rump	Roast at 300°	45 to 55 minutes per pound well
Top round ½ inch	Broil	10 to 12 minutes per steak rare
		12 to 15 minutes per steak medium
Pot roast	Braise, stew	45 to 55 minutes per pound well

FOOD	METHOD	TIME
Steaks 2 inches	Broil	45 to 50 minutes per steak rare
		60 to 80 minutes per steak medium
Steaks 1 inch	Broil	20 to 25 minutes per steak rare
		30 to 40 minutes per steak medium
Hamburger 1 inch	Broil	20 to 25 minutes rare
		25 to 30 minutes medium
	Panbroil	10 to 14 minutes rare
		12 to 15 minutes medium
Lamb		
Rolled shoulder	Roast at 300°	50 to 55 minutes per pound
Leg of lamb, whole and		
cushion shoulder	Roast at 300°	40 to 45 minutes per pound
Chops 2 inches	Broil	26 to 30 minutes
Chops 1 inch	Broil	15 to 18 minutes
Pork		
Center cut roast	Roast at 350°	45 to 50 minutes per pound
Rolled shoulder	Roast at 350°	50 to 60 minutes per pound
Whole loin	Roast at 350°	25 to 35 minutes per pound
End	Roast at 350°	60 to 70 minutes per pound
Cushion shoulder	Roast at 350°	45 to 55 minutes per pound
Chops	Braise	55 to 65 minutes
Spareribs	Roast at 350°	40 to 45 minutes per pound
Fresh ham butt	Roast at 350°	45 to 55 minutes per pound
Smoked whole, large	Roast at 350°	25 to 35 minutes per pound
Medium, small or half	Roast at 350°	35 to 45 minutes per pound
Ham steaks 1 inch	Broil	30 to 45 minutes per steak
Veal		
Leg	Roast at 300°	40 to 50 minutes per pound
Loin	Roast at 300°	50 to 60 minutes per pound
Shoulder, rolled	Roast at 300°	55 to 60 minutes per pound
Cushion shoulder	Roast at 300°	50 to 60 minutes per pound
Breast, rolled	Roast at 300°	50 to 60 minutes per pound
Chops	Braise	55 to 65 minutes
Cutlets	Braise	45 to 55 minutes
Vegetables		See page 50
Prepared combination dishes	Double boiler	30 minutes per pint
Prepared combination dishes	Bake at 400°	45 to 60 minutes per pint
		65 to 125 minutes per quart
Pies, unbaked	Start in a 450°	15 to 20 minutes
	oven, reduce	
	to 375°	40 to 45 minutes
Rolled cookies	Bake at 350°	10 to 12 minutes
	to 375°	

Defrosting Frozen Foods

Because of the great variance in equipment and weather conditions, a general rule for defrosting of frozen foods is a great deal more satisfactory than specific times for every type of food.

How long it takes for any given food to defrost depends on what temperature it was before it was taken from the freezer; on the location in which you place it in the refrigerator (if defrosting in the refrigerator); on the temperature of the refrigerator; on how many times the refrigerator is opened; on the weather outside.

A good general rule to follow for defrosting in the refrigerator would be: at 40 degrees allow about six hours per pound.

For defrosting at room temperature the general rule is about three hours per pound.

Unless you are home to watch poultry or fish, it is better to defrost them in the refrigerator where they will stay cold once they have defrosted.

Vegetables should be cooked frozen (see p. 50).

The following items defrost at a rate very unlike meat and poultry:

FOOD	TIME IN REFRIGERATOR	TIME AT ROOM TEMPERATURE
Baked goods		
Breads		1 hour
Rolls		1 hour
Cakes, single layer		1 to 1½ hours
Cakes, whole 2-layer		2 to 3 hours
angel and sponge		2 hours
Cupcakes		15 to 25 minutes
Cookies		15 minutes
Pies (served cold)		6 hours
Pie shells		10 to 20 minutes
Unbaked goods		
Cake batter		1½ hours
Yeast breads		250° oven 45 minutes
Yeast rolls		Covered, warm place 2 to 4 hours then bake both as usual
Sandwiches		2 to 3 hours
Canapés		½ to 1 hour
Dips	24 hours	5 to 6 hours

FOOD	TIME IN REFRIGERATOR	TIME AT ROOM TEMPERATURE
Cream	24 hours	
Eggs	24 hours	
Steamed puddings		6 hours—then steam at 300° 20 to 30 minutes
Cheese	5 hours	
Butter, 1 pound	5 hours	

What Not to Freeze

There are very few foods that do not take to freezing so we will discuss the "don'ts" first. In the section entitled "Feasible Freezables," we will go into detail about some of the foods you probably have never dreamed of freezing.

Fresh Raw Vegetables cannot be frozen with the exception of green peppers, cabbage and celery. Cabbage and celery wilt, of course, upon defrosting, but are perfect for cooked dishes.

Hard-cooked Eggs become tough, but ground whites can be frozen and used for garnish.

Boiled White Potatoes become mealy.

Boiled Frostings turn sticky.

Gelatin Dishes—most of them weep.

Sour Cream separates.

Melon Balls can be and are commercially frozen, but we frankly do not like their appearance or texture after defrosting.

Corn on the Cob—Ditto.

Bananas *

Mayonnaise

Custard and Cream Pies

Macaroons

Stuffed poultry is frozen by commercial packers but we do not suggest it in a home freezer. It is difficult to get the inside of a large stuffed bird frozen solid and consequently bacteria can form. However, there would be no harm in freezing one for two or three days if you chill the stuffing first. It is safe to freeze small stuffed birds such as squabs and Rock Cornish hens. Except for these few things, everything else is freezable.

* There is a popular belief that bananas should not be refrigerated. We find that, although the banana peel becomes discolored with refrigeration, the fruit itself remains firm, white and flavorful much longer.

BLANCHING OF VEGETABLES AND FREEZING OF VEGETABLES AND FRUITS

Vegetables

Select young tender, garden-fresh vegetables.

Wash vegetables in cold water, trim according to directions below.

Blanch. (Parboil or pour boiling water over food, then drain and rinse with cold water in order to stop enzyme action, which is aging the vegetable.) This applies to all vegetables with exceptions that will be noted. Each pound of prepared vegetables requires at least one gallon of boiling water.

Use blancher or large kettle, with cover, into which wire basket fits.

Count blanching time when water returns to boil after adding vegetables.

Cool immediately by plunging vegetables into ice water.

Dry pack in plastic containers or bags, allowing head space.

Cook frozen. See p. 50.

VEGETABLE	HOW TO PREPARE FOR FREEZING
Artichokes	Pull off coarse outer leaves. Trim tops and stems. Blanch 8 to 10 minutes. Add ½ cup lemon juice to every 2 quarts water.
Asparagus	Trim off tough portion of stalk. Blanch 2 to 4 minutes depending on thickness of stalk.
Beans, green or wax	Trim ends. Cut into 1-inch or 2-inch pieces or french. Blanch 1½ minutes.
Beans, lima	Remove from pods. Sort for size. Blanch 2 to 3 minutes, depending on size.
Beets	Small whole: Peel and blanch 5 minutes. Mature large: Cook until tender, 45 to 50 minutes. Peel, slice or dice.
Broccoli	Trim off woodiness and large leaves. Cut into serving pieces. Split large stalks to ½-inch thickness. Blanch 2 to 3 minutes.
Brussels sprouts	Trim outer leaves. Blanch 3 to 4 minutes.

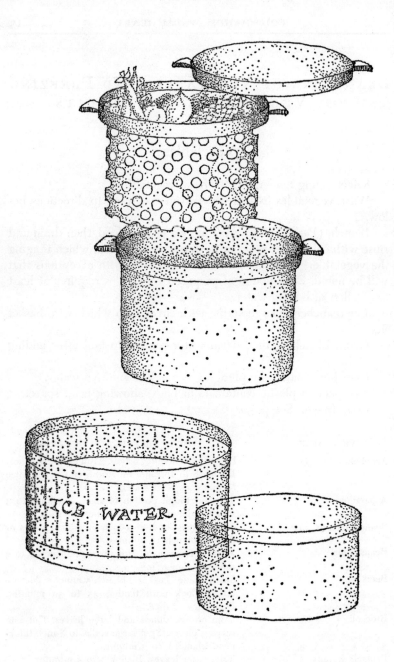

VEGETABLE	HOW TO PREPARE FOR FREEZING
Cabbage	Suitable only for cooked dishes. Trim coarse outer leaves. Coarse shred or separate leaves. Blanch 1½ minutes.
Carrots	Scrape, cut in ⅓-inch dice. Blanch 2½ minutes. Small whole carrots: Blanch 3 to 5 minutes.
Cauliflower	Break into serving pieces. Blanch 3 minutes.
Celery	Trim, cut into 1-inch lengths. Blanch 3 minutes. Suitable only for cooked dishes.
Celery root	Wash and trim. Cook until almost tender. Peel and slice.
Chestnuts	Boil, drain and shell.
Chives	Chop. Do not blanch.
Corn *	Husk and de-silk. On the cob: Blanch 5 to 8 minutes. Cut corn: Blanch on cob 1½ minutes. Chill, then cut kernels from cob.
Eggplant	Peel, cut in ⅓-inch slices or dice. Blanch 4 minutes, then dip in ⅓ cup lemon juice mixed with 2½ pints cold water.
Fennel	Trim, cut in 1-inch lengths. Blanch 3 minutes.
Green peppers	Wash, remove seeds and stem; chop. Do not blanch.
Kohlrabi	Small roots, 2 to 3 inches in diameter. Cut off tops, peel and dice. Blanch 1½ minutes.
Mushrooms	Rinse and dry on paper toweling. Trim end of stem. Do not blanch. Use in cooked dishes. Do not defrost completely and they will slice more easily.
Okra	Cut off stems. Small pods: Blanch 2 minutes. Large pods: Blanch 3 minutes.
Onions	Peel and chop. Do not blanch.
Parsley	Chop. Do not blanch.
Parsnips	Cut off tops, peel. Cut into ½-inch cubes or slices. Blanch 2 minutes.
Peas	Black-eyed: Shell, blanch 2 minutes. Green: Shell, blanch ½ to 1 minute.
Pumpkin	Seed and quarter. Cook until soft. Remove pulp and mash.
Rutabagas	Cut off tops, peel and dice. Blanch 1 minute.
Soybeans	Blanch in pod 4 to 5 minutes. Cool and squeeze beans from pod.
Spinach	Blanch 1½ minutes.
(beet greens, chard, collards,	Collards: 3 minutes. Other greens: 2 minutes.

* It is against our better judgment to freeze corn on the cob. The loss of flavor and tenderness is not worth the effort.

VEGETABLE	HOW TO PREPARE FOR FREEZING
kale, mustard greens, turnip greens)	
Squash, summer varieties	Cut in ½-inch slices. Blanch 3 minutes.
Squash, winter	Cut into pieces, seed. Cook until tender. Remove pulp and mash.
Sweet potatoes	Cook until almost tender. Cool and peel. Dip whole or sliced in solution of ½ cup lemon juice to 1 quart water for 5 seconds or add 2 tablespoons orange or lemon juice to each quart of mashed.
Tomatoes, juice	Trim and quarter. Simmer 5 to 10 minutes. Press through sieve. May be seasoned with 1 teaspoon salt to each quart juice.
Tomatoes, pureed	Trim and quarter. Simmer until they can be forced through a strainer. May be seasoned with salt, 1 teaspoon per quart.
Tomatoes, stewed	Peel and quarter. Cook 10 to 20 minutes.
Turnips	Peel, cut into ½-inch cubes. Blanch 2 minutes.
Water chestnuts	Peel. Do not blanch.

Fruits

Select firm texture, mature fruits. Prepare to freeze immediately after harvesting. Certain varieties freeze more successfully than others but if freshly picked and carefully handled, most fruits will freeze satisfactorily.

Wash thoroughly in cold water. Cut and trim according to directions below.

Pack in "Cold Syrup," "Sugar Pack" or "Unsweetened Pack."

Cold Syrups

PERCENT	SUGAR IN CUPS	WATER IN CUPS
30	2	4
40	3	4
50	4¾	4

Cold Syrup

Follow the above table for percent of cold syrup called for in directions, dissolving sugar in cold or hot water. If hot water is used, cool syrup. The syrup may be made up beforehand and refrigerated. To insure that the syrup covers all the fruit, press a crumpled piece of freezer paper on top and press down fruit into syrup before sealing lid.

Sugar Pack

See instructions below for amount of sugar needed for each fruit. Mix sugar gently with fruit until it is dissolved. Press crumpled piece of freezer paper on top of fruit to keep fruit covered. Make a note on the container of amount of sugar used.

Unsweetened Pack

Dry pack or cover with water containing required amount of ascorbic acid, given in directions.

Ascorbic acid is needed to prevent some light fruits—those shown below—from darkening and losing flavor. However, if cold fresh fruit is cut directly into cold syrup and covered with it, then frozen at once, there should be little darkening without the ascorbic acid.

For dry pack use rigid containers or plastic bags. "Head" room is not needed. Fruits frozen by other methods should be packed in rigid containers, allowing a half inch to one and a half inches of headroom.

Fruits to be served without cooking should not be completely thawed. A few ice crystals in them keep them from going limp and enhance their flavor.

FRUITS	HOW TO PREPARE FOR FREEZING
Apples (with the exception of Red Delicious)	For pies: Peel, core, slice. Drop in boiling 30 percent syrup, scald 2 minutes. Lift from syrup, drain and pack.
Apricots	Plunge into boiling water for 30 seconds to loosen skins; peel. Cut in half or slice into 40 percent cold syrup with ¼ teaspoon ascorbic acid per quart syrup. Puree: Quarter, heat to boiling in just enough water to prevent scorching; sieve. 1 cup sugar for each quart and ¼ teaspoon ascorbic acid dissolved in ¼ cup water.

FRUITS	HOW TO PREPARE FOR FREEZING
Avocados	Peel, mash. Add 3 tablespoons lemon juice per quart.
Berries (blackberries, blueberries, raspberries, boysenberries, cranberries, elderberries, gooseberries, strawberries, huckleberries, dewberries, loganberries, youngberries and currants)	All may be frozen dry pack method. Sort and stem. Spread on trays until frozen, then pack. Syrup pack: Use 50 percent cold syrup for gooseberries, cranberries and currants. Use 40 percent syrup for all others.
Cherries, sour	Sort, pit if desired. Mix with dry sugar (1 pound sugar to 5 pounds cherries) until dissolved.
Cherries, sweet	Sort, pit if desired. Cover with 40 percent cold syrup mixed with ½ teaspoon ascorbic acid per quart of syrup.
Coconut, fresh	Shred, add coconut milk. To use, pour off milk. Or toast coconut and freeze. Use toasted in 2 months.
Dates	Pit if desired. Dry pack.
Figs	Sort, stem, peel and slice. Use 30 percent cold syrup or dry pack. Dry pack dried figs.
Grapefruit	Peel, remove membranes and seeds. Pack in 40 percent cold syrup made with juice from fruit (do not heat) or dry pack. Juice: Squeeze and sweeten with 2 tablespoons sugar per quart. Freeze in glass containers.
Grapes	Stem. Leave seedless grapes whole. Halve and seed others. Pack in 30 percent cold syrup.
Kumquats	Pack in 30 percent cold syrup or dry pack.
Lemons and Limes	Squeeze juice, freeze in ice cube trays. Remove frozen cubes to plastic bags.
Melons *	Seed, ball, cube or slice into 30 percent cold syrup. Add 1 teaspoon lemon juice to each cup syrup.
Nectarines	Peel, if desired. Sort, pit, quarter, halve or slice into 40 percent cold syrup with ½ teaspoon ascorbic acid per quart syrup.
Oranges (except navel)	Prepare and pack as grapefruit or squeeze for juice, add sugar if desired and freeze as lemon juice.

* We don't recommend freezing melons because they lose a great deal of flavor and all their crispness when thawed.

FRUITS	HOW TO PREPARE FOR FREEZING
Peaches	Sort, pit and chill. Peel without scalding, if possible. Halve, quarter or slice into 40 percent cold syrup with ½ teaspoon ascorbic acid per quart syrup.
Pears	Peel, halve or quarter and core. Heat in boiling 40 percent syrup 1 to 2 minutes depending on size of fruit. Drain and cool. Pack in 40 percent cold syrup with ¾ teaspoon ascorbic acid per quart of syrup.
Persimmons	Peel. Pack in 30 percent cold syrup with 1 tablespoon lemon juice per 5 cups syrup. Puree: Peel and press through sieve. To each quart puree add ⅛ teaspoon ascorbic acid. Pack unsweetened or add 1 cup sugar to each 4 cups puree.
Pineapple	Peel, core, slice, dice, crush or cut into wedges or sticks. Pack in 30 percent cold syrup or dry pack.
Plums	Sort. Halve or quarter if desired. Pit. Pack in 40 percent cold syrup with ½ teaspoon ascorbic acid per quart syrup. Dried prunes may be dry packed.
Raisins	Dry pack.
Rhubard	Trim, cut into desired lengths. To retain flavor heat in boiling water 1 minute and quick cool. Pack in 40 percent cold syrup or dry pack.

PACKAGING AND LABELING

And now a most important topic on the agenda—wrapping for freezing. It is important to wrap properly to prevent foods from changing color, freezer burning, dehydrating and generally decreasing in quality. As you wrap, especially when using containers and bags, squeeze out as much air as possible. Pack semisolid foods tightly, leaving no air holes. Air dries out food. When using papers, be sure to protect the foods completely, wrapping securely. Be sure no strange odors can enter the package. The packing materials must be moistureproof and vaporproof.

Because of the multiplicity of available materials and the fact that they are constantly being changed or added to, it is difficult to keep up to date. Between the time of writing of this book and the time you are reading this particular paragraph, new packaging materials may become available for the home freezer which will make this whole section obsolete.

Be certain that the packaging materials you buy are freezer weight.

For wrapping there is heavy-duty aluminum foil, thermoplastic, cellophane, polyethylene, coated and laminated paper.

There are reusable polyethylene bags.

Wrap either in butcher's or drug store wrap (Illustrations # 2, 3).

Glass jars are handy for soups, fruit juices and other liquids and are, of course, reusable, though breakable. Freezing itself will not break the glass, however.

Plastic containers with plastic lids and heavy waxed cartons with waxed lids are extremely useful, reusable and unbreakable. For positive protection seal lid to container with freezer tape. For ease in separation you may divide portions of semiliquid or solid food, sorted in large containers, with double thicknesses of aluminum foil or cellophane. Remember to leave ¼- to 1-inch headroom for expansion.

Preformed containers are available in aluminum foil and are both heatable and reusable.

There are now on the market casseroles and dishes that can go from freezer to oven to table.

New products include sturdy bags of transparent plastic that stand up to temperatures from zero to boiling. The advantage here is that they save pot-watching as well as pot-washing for the frozen foods go directly from the freezer into a pot of boiling water. There is a heat sealing machine on the market for this kind of packaging.

There are also plastic bags by the roll which snap apart into one-bag sections. These are really handy for freezing quantities of sandwiches, but their thinness keeps their life-span short. Don't forget the new coffee cans with plastic covers and the many reusable containers of commercially frozen foods.

For securing wrappings, freezer tape, scotch tape, plastic covered wire ties, pipe cleaners, plastic fasteners and rubber bands are available.

A felt-tipped marking pen is perfect for writing on aluminum foil and plastic containers and can be distinguished quite readily.

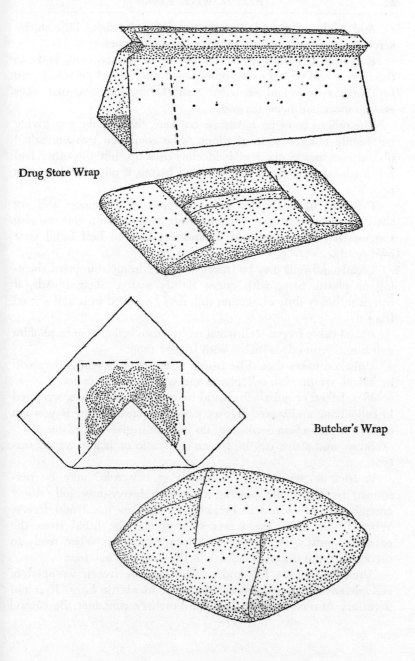

Drug Store Wrap

Butcher's Wrap

And while we are talking about marking, let these little stories serve as a warning against freezing unlabeled packages.

Earlier in our freezing careers one of us dashed confidently to the freezer and pulled out goodies when unexpected guests arrived for dinner, only to find out when it was far too late, that two cakes and no meat had been thawed.

The other one of us, not to be outdone, thought she was giving her family chicken soup at dinner. She combined two unmarked plastic containers: one had held chicken soup, but the other had fish stock—at least that's how it tasted before it all went down the drain!

Different foods require different types of containers and we shall try to suggest what is appropriate and efficient. But we also suggest that you experiment to find out how to best fulfill your own needs.

Breads and rolls may be frozen wrapped in moistureproof sheeting or plastic bags, with edges tightly sealed. Some breads, if frozen in heavy-duty aluminum foil, may be baked in it and served from it.

Baked cakes freeze well when wrapped in cellophane or pliofilm and boxed with edges sealed with freezer tape.

Unbaked cakes should be frozen in the pans in which they will be baked, wrapped in cellophane and waxed freezer paper.

Pies, baked or unbaked, should be frozen in pie plates, wrapped in cellophane and waxed freezer paper or plastic bags. If you are to bake a pie before defrosting, do not use a glass pie plate.

Stews and sauce can be frozen in plastic or heavy waxed cartons.

A trick known as the "disappearing casserole" may be performed by lining the cooking dish with heavy-duty foil. Allow enough to fold over, too. Prepare casserole as usual and freeze. When frozen solid, the wrapped food may be lifted from the casserole, putting the utensil back into circulation. When ready to serve, place the frozen dish back in the original container.

Uncooked meats, fish and poultry may be frozen wrapped in cellophane and waxed freezer paper or in plastic bags. It is not necessary to remove meat from the butcher's container. Be careful

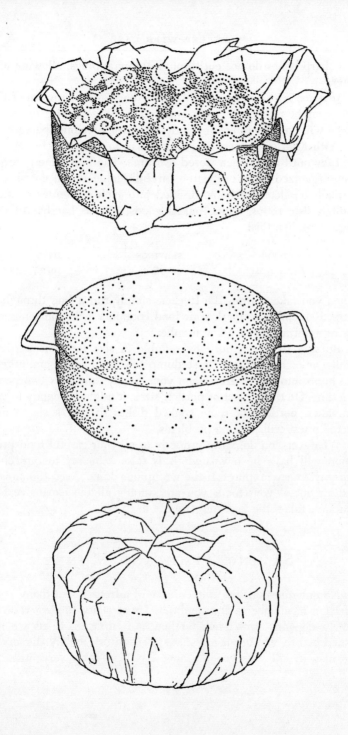

that sharp bones do not cut through the wrappings, allowing air to enter.

If space is at a premium, fill plastic bags and fit several of them into straight-sided cake pans and freeze. When solid, the square shape will pack more conveniently into ever precious space.

With a large freezer, it is quite easy to "lose" or forget some delicacy until it has been stored overtime. The best remedy for this is an organized inventory of the carefully labeled and dated foods. A small looseleaf notebook, divided into such categories as meats, poultry, fish, soups, fruits, baked goods, etc., is handy. An entry might look like this:

FOOD	SERVINGS	DATE
Rump roast	6	10/24

When you take it from the freezer, simply run a line through the entry. Remember to mark your food container with the same identifying information or a key number.

Be sure to freeze portions suitable in size for your particular family or company use. Don't dump ten pounds of hamburger in one lump into the freezer when your family only uses two pounds at a time. On the subject of portion sizes, it might be handy to wrap individual portions of some cooked dishes so that a single unexpected guest will pose no problems.

Whatever you do, wrap properly or all your careful food preparation will have been wasted. It is false economy to buy cheap, flimsy freezer wrappings. If the wrappings do not keep the moisture and air out of your foods you are ruining all the expensive foods you have taken the time and trouble to freeze.

SAVING TIME AND MONEY

No one questions the convenience of a freezer, but many people question its money saving qualities. Its capacity to save time and money depends very much on how it is utilized. If, as we mentioned before, you use it merely as a repository for TV dinners and the like, it will save you no money and probably very little time.

However, it can, with a minimum of last-minute effort, make you a gourmet cook and a thrifty gourmet in the bargain.

When mushrooms are 39¢ a pound instead of 69¢—or nonexistent—you can stock up. When blueberries make their seasonal appearance, freeze your own for winter use instead of depending on the more expensive commercially frozen ones. Most meats and poultry vary widely in price throughout the year. When chicken prices plunge downward, buy a dozen or more. It is difficult for some people to get used to the idea of buying in large quantities and the initial investment may hurt! But if you really care to keep an accurate check over a year's time, you will find that a few pennies here and there add up so that slowly but surely the freezer and its operation will pay for themselves. Depending on your particular family's needs, you will find many ways to make those pennies count. For greatest economy keep rotating your frozen foods so that the oldest are used first. Do not keep them any longer than necessary. In another section we discuss the thrifty and tasty utilization of leftovers (certainly a money saver), which often ended up in the garbage before the days of the freezer.

Time, another precious commodity in our busy world, can be saved by putting the new "servant" in your house to work.

Shopping trips may be cut down.

Baking time may be reduced. You will soon see how timesaving it is to bake six pies instead of one, since you take out the utensils and dirty the kitchen only once. You also economize on fuel, since at least two pies can bake at a time in one oven. This is equally true of preparing large quantities of stew, casseroles, cookies, etc.

In addition, isn't it lovely to whip out that pie or beef stroganoff or cheese hors d'oeuvre without having devoted hours to its preparation at serving time? In this way a freezer is a "silent servant" in your home—and one that isn't likely to quit!

Now, can you truthfully say you lived happily without owning a freezer? We think not and on that assumption have written this book. It's dedicated to all of you who share our admiration for this most marvelous home appliance.

2

Cooking After Five

Cooking After Five

THE WORKING HOUSEWIFE

Now that we have determined once and for all that you will have a freezer, and you have run right out and bought one, the question is, how do you fill it?

In the beginning this takes time, so be patient. Anyway, the family budget could not be stretched enough to fill it all in one week. But in two months you should have enough supplies salted away to meet all emergencies with great aplomb.

The question is one of time or lack of it. This is especially true for the working housewife, and there are so many in today's society. Although she may work from 7:30 to 3:30 or 9:00 to 5:00 she must still go home and prepare dinner. When can she do it?

The freezer, properly used by the working girl, can be her very best friend in the kitchen. She can treat her family to a variety of menus and save herself a great deal of that precious commodity, time.

P.S. Even if you don't work (outside your home that is) these suggestions should be equally valuable for you.

FREEZE IT NOW, SERVE IT LATER

Cooking a Week at a Time

Whether you work and can devote only a few hours a week to cooking or whether you simply like to spend as little time as possible in the kitchen, the freeze-it-now-serve-it-later plan should be right up your alley.

It takes very little more effort to make these dishes for twelve or sixteen servings than for six or eight. And once the kitchen is a wreck, why not cook up a few other dishes to tuck away in the freezer? Your dinners will taste much better than anything you can buy from the shelves or frozen food cabinets of your supermarket and doubtless they will cost less, too.

The menus following are suggestions for family dinners Monday through Friday. They presuppose that you have done your home-work and that your freezer is already filled with goodies. If not, what better time to begin!

WEEK I
MONDAY
TOMATO JUICE
* HAM LOAF VAN ALLEN
* FROZEN HORSERADISH RELISH
FROZEN STRING BEANS
COOKIES

HAM LOAF VAN ALLEN
(12 to 16 servings)

Combine

3 pounds ground ham	24 saltines, rolled fine
3 pounds ground pork	2 cans condensed tomato soup
4 eggs	

Divide ingredients into four bread-loaf pans and freeze in portions suitable for your family. To serve, defrost and bake at 375° for 1½ hours. This is also delicious served cold.

FROZEN HORSERADISH RELISH

Whip

2 cups heavy cream

Fold in

2 cups creamed cottage cheese	3 tablespoons vinegar
6 tablespoons chopped chives	4 teaspoons sugar
1 cup freshly grated horseradish	Salt to taste

Pour mixture into ice-cube trays, set divider in place. Freeze. When relish is frozen, pop out cubes and package in plastic bag. To serve, place frozen cubes in lettuce cups or lemon shells.

TUESDAY
Grapefruit Halves
* Pot Roast
* Individual Potato Puddings
Frozen Peas
Ice Cream

POT ROAST
(1½ to 2 servings per pound)

In a heavy kettle, brown slowly in its own fat a 6- to 8-pound brisket, well salted. Add 4 to 6 onions, chopped, and cook until limp.

Reduce heat to low and cover. As the meat cooks slowly it will make its own gravy. For a 6-pound brisket cook about 4 hours. (If this is not enough you may finish cooking when you reheat it.) Cool quickly. Slice the meat, dividing into portions suitable for your family. Freeze in its own gravy. (This is one dish that improves with reheating.) To serve, defrost and place in baking dish; bake at 350° for 1 hour, basting if necessary. Adjust seasonings.

INDIVIDUAL POTATO PUDDINGS
(16 servings)

Peel and grate

12 medium potatoes

Allow to drain. Discard liquid. Add to potatoes

2 onions, grated	4 eggs, well beaten

Combine and add to potatoes

1 cup flour
1 tablespoon salt

1 teaspoon baking powder
½ teaspoon pepper

Add

8 tablespoons melted chicken fat or butter

Spoon into greased medium-sized muffin tins. Fill to top. Bake at 375° for 1 hour, until brown and crusty. Allow to stand on counter a few minutes then run knife around edge to remove from pan. Freeze. To serve, reheat wrapped in foil in 350° oven.

WEDNESDAY

* MINESTRONE
* FROZEN HAMBURGER SURPRISE
PEAS SUPRÊME (p. 57)
FROZEN FRENCH FRIES
FRUIT IN SEASON

MINESTRONE

(6 quarts)

Brown in deep kettle

¼ pound bacon, diced

2 onions, sliced

Add

2 cups chopped cabbage
1 cup chopped escarole
1 cup chopped celery
2 carrots, sliced

½ cup chopped parsley
1 clove garlic
12 cups water

Simmer 40 minutes. Then add

1 #2 can navy beans, drained
1 #2 can chick peas, drained
1 #2 can tomatoes

1 tablespoon oregano
1 teaspoon basil
1½ tablespoons salt

Bring to a boil. Cover and simmer 10 minutes. Add 1 cup macaroni. Cook 10 minutes or until macaroni is almost tender. Chill quickly; freeze. To serve, defrost completely, heat if necessary to remove from container. Heat slowly until dissolved; adjust seasonings.

HAMBURGER SURPRISE

Before freezing patties, make a thin patty. On it put 1 slice or piece of Cheddar cheese. Top with another thin patty and seal. Cheese melts as hamburger cooks.

THURSDAY

* LAMB CHOPS IN BARBECUE SAUCE
RICE
MIXED SALAD
CINNAMON HORNS (p. 114)

LAMB CHOPS IN BARBECUE SAUCE

(16 servings)

Brown in their own fat

  32 lamb chops

Drain off drippings. Combine chops with

4 cups catsup	4 lemons, thinly sliced
4 cups chili sauce	2 tablespoons plus 2 teaspoons
2 cups brown sugar	Worcestershire sauce
2 cups vinegar	2 tablespoons lemon juice
8 large onions, sliced	1 teaspoon pepper

Chill quickly and freeze in portions suitable for your family's use. To serve, defrost and cook chops in sauce over low heat 45 to 60 minutes; adjust seasonings.

FRIDAY

* SALMON LOAF
PARSLEY POTATOES
GREEN BEANS CHILI (p. 55)
SOUR CREAM COFFEE CAKE (p. 120)

SALMON LOAF
(10 to 12 servings)

Bone and flake

  4 1-pound cans salmon

Add and mix thoroughly

  4 eggs, slightly beaten   4 tablespoons melted butter
  2 cups milk   ½ cup chopped parsley
  2 cups crushed potato chips

Place in two greased 2-quart loaf pans and freeze. To serve, defrost and bake at 400° for 30 minutes.

WEEK II
MONDAY
TOMATO JUICE
* SWISS MEAT ROLL
BAKED POTATOES
FROZEN ASPARAGUS
OATMEAL TOLL HOUSE COOKIES (p. 118)

SWISS MEAT ROLL
(10 to 12 servings)

Season well, mix as usual and shape into 4 loaves

  4 pounds ground beef

Flatten each loaf on waxed paper and shape into rectangle.

Cover each rectangle with

  6 to 8 slices Swiss cheese

Roll up as for jelly roll.

Cover with

  4 8-ounce cans tomato sauce

Freeze. To serve, defrost and bake at 350° for 45 minutes.

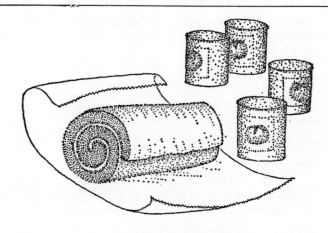

TUESDAY
* Veal Birds with Apples
Rice
Green Salad
Ice Cream

VEAL BIRDS WITH APPLES
(12 servings)

Melt in large skillet

¾ cup butter or margarine

Add and sauté until golden

3 cups finely chopped onion

Add

7½ cups soft bread cubes	1 tablespoon salt
3 cups coarsely chopped, peeled apples	½ tablespoon poultry seasoning

Cook stirring over medium heat about 6 minutes.

Divide and pound into 36 thin scallops

4½ pounds veal

Place 1 heaping tablespoon stuffing on each veal scallop. Roll up and secure with wooden picks.

Dredge each roll in

   5 tablespoons flour

Heat in skillet

   6 tablespoons butter

Brown rolls well on all sides. Add

   3¼ cups apple cider

Freeze in portions suitable for your family. To serve, defrost and simmer rolls 30 to 35 minutes in cider in covered skillet. Remove picks, adjust seasonings, then spoon juices over veal and serve.

WEDNESDAY
* Hungarian Goulash
Frozen String Beans
Rolls
Cinnamon Horns (p. 114)

HUNGARIAN GOULASH
(12 servings)

Combine and brown

   4 pounds stew beef (chuck, round steak, etc.) cut in 2-inch cubes
   4 tablespoons fat

Season with

   Salt, pepper and paprika

Stir well and add

   4 cloves garlic, minced   1 cup water
   2 cans tomato paste   8 allspice cloves

Simmer covered about 2 hours. Chill quickly and freeze in portions suitable for your family. To serve, defrost, adjust seasonings and cook 15 minutes.

Then add

  1 large peeled and quartered potato per serving

Simmer an additional 45 minutes, or until tender.

THURSDAY
Fruit Cup
* Moussaka
Rice
Lettuce and Tomato
Ice Cream

MOUSSAKA
(12 servings)

Brown

3 pounds ground chuck	3 tablespoons butter

Add

3 onions, chopped	½ teaspoon cinnamon
6 tablespoons tomato paste	½ teaspoon nutmeg
½ cup (or more) dry red wine	½ teaspoon pepper
½ cup chopped parsley	1½ teaspoons salt

Cook 3 minutes. Cool. Then melt

  6 tablespoons butter

Take from heat. Stir in

6 tablespoons flour	3 cups milk

Return to low heat, stir until smooth. Take from heat, cool slightly. Add

  6 egg yolks, beaten

Wash and slice (but do not peel), then brown in butter

  6 medium eggplants

In casserole arrange layers of eggplant, meat and sauce. Sprinkle each layer with

3 tablespoons bread crumbs	¾ cup grated Parmesan cheese

End with sauce. Freeze. To serve, defrost and top with

  6 tablespoons bread crumbs   1½ cups grated Parmesan cheese

Bake 45 to 60 minutes at 375°.

FRIDAY
Soup
* Orange-Glazed Chicken
Baked Potato
Green Salad
Heat-and-Serve Rolls
Apricot Crescents and Sherbet (p. 193)

ORANGE-GLAZED CHICKEN
(12 servings)

Marinate for at least 1 hour

  3 2½- to 3-pound broilers, cut into serving pieces

in

  1½ cups French dressing

Brown chickens under the broiler.

Heat together

  3 7-ounce bottles ginger ale   1 tablespoon cornstarch
  1½ cups orange juice

Using this as a glaze, pour over chicken. Freeze. To serve, defrost and
bake chicken at 300° for 1½ hours, basting with the glaze.

WEEK III
MONDAY
Fruit Juice
* Polish Pork Chops
Broad Egg Noodles
Frozen Broccoli
Toffee Squares (p. 121)

POLISH PORK CHOPS
(12 servings)

Brown in skillet on both sides

24 pork chops

Cover, reduce heat and cook slowly, about 15 minutes.

Add

¾ cup chopped onion   3 8-ounce cans tomato paste

Chill quickly and freeze in portions suitable for your family. To serve, defrost and cook for 15 minutes, until chops are tender and heated through.

Add for every 4 servings

½ cup sour cream

Simmer and stir in

3 tablespoons dry sherry   Salt and pepper to taste
1 small dill pickle, chopped

TUESDAY
* PICADILLO
SPAGHETTI
GREEN SALAD
ITALIAN BREAD
POUND CAKE (p. 99)

PICADILLO
(12 servings)

Sauté until brown

3 pounds ground chuck   ¾ cup diced green pepper
3 small onions, diced   ½ cup olive oil
3 cloves garlic, stuck on wooden
   picks

Remove garlic and add

3 cups canned tomatoes
3 8-ounce cans tomato sauce
3 tablespoons vinegar
1 tablespoon sugar
1 tablespoon salt

4 bay leaves
3 tablespoons capers
¾ teaspoon oregano
1½ cups raisins

Chill quickly and freeze in portions suitable for your family. To serve, defrost, simmer 30 minutes in covered pot. Serve with spaghetti.

WEDNESDAY

MINESTRONE
EYE-OF-THE-ROUND ROAST
* EGGPLANT
* CARAWAY CHEESE BREAD
FRESH FRUIT

EGGPLANT
(12 servings)

In a skillet heat

½ cup olive oil

Stir in, cooking over low heat until they begin to brown

4 green peppers, minced
4 eggplants, pared and cut in 1-inch dice

2 cloves garlic, sliced
2 large onions, minced

Stir in

2 16-ounce cans Spanish-style tomato sauce
4 teaspoons salt

1½ teaspoons freshly ground pepper
2 teaspoons brown sugar

Cook slowly until eggplant is tender. Chill quickly and freeze in portions suitable for your family.

To serve, defrost and add for every 4 servings

¼ cup grated Parmesan cheese

Heat through for about 15 minutes.

You may make a main dish out of this by adding

1 pound ground chuck, browned, per four servings

CARAWAY CHEESE BREAD
(8 to 12 servings)

Split lengthwise

2 long loaves French bread

Mix together and spread cut sides of bread with

1 pound grated Cheddar cheese   2 tablespoons caraway seeds
½ cup butter

Freeze. To serve, defrost and cut into serving pieces; broil until cheese is bubbly.

THURSDAY
* Lamb Chops in Sour Cream
Macaroni
Lettuce and Tomato
Ice Cream

LAMB CHOPS IN SOUR CREAM
(10 to 12 servings)

Rub

18 shoulder lamb chops

with

Cut garlic cloves

Brown in

½ cup oil

Divide into suitable-sized casseroles. Into pan drippings stir

3 cups sour cream   1½ teaspoons salt
3 tablespoons vinegar   ¾ teaspoon pepper
3 tablespoons Worcestershire   Paprika
   sauce

Pour over meat. Arrange on top of each casserole

2 bay leaves

Freeze in portions suitable for your family. To serve, defrost and bake at 350° for 50 to 60 minutes.

FRIDAY
JUICE OR GRAPEFRUIT
* SHRIMP À LA NORMAN
TOAST POINTS
FROZEN PEAS
SHERBET AND COOKIES

SHRIMP À LA NORMAN
(12 servings)

Melt

6 tablespoons butter

Add

1¼ pound fresh mushrooms,   3 small cloves garlic, crushed
quartered

Cover and sauté gently for 5 minutes. Then add

1 tablespoon grated onion

Cover and cook 5 minutes longer. Add

6 cups canned tomatoes   ¾ teaspoon paprika
¼ teaspoon baking soda   Salt and pepper to taste
1½ teaspoons sugar

Simmer 15 minutes. Blend to a smooth paste

1 cup heavy cream   ½ cup plus 1 tablespoon flour

To this paste add

1⅛ cups dry sherry   12 to 16 drops Angostura bitters
4½ tablespoon Worcestershire
sauce

Pour the sherry-cream mixture into the tomato-mushroom mixture, stirring to make smooth. Cook 3 minutes. Add

6 cups peeled, cooked shrimp   3 tablespoons chopped parsley

Divide into suitable portions and freeze. To serve, defrost, pour into casseroles, sprinkle each four servings with

¼ cup bread crumbs

Dot each 4 servings with

1½ tablespoons butter

Bake at 375° for 25 to 35 minutes, depending on size of casserole. Serve immediately on toast points.

WEEK IV
MONDAY
MELON
* MEAT LOAF RING
MASHED POTATOES
FROZEN SPINACH
SCHNECKEN (p. 198)

MEAT LOAF RING
(12 to 16 servings)

Grease well two 2-quart ring molds. Line with

8 slices bacon

Grind

2 cups raw carrot   2 cups raw potato

Sauté

1½ cups onion, minced   4 pounds ground chuck
1 pound mushrooms, sliced

Combine above ingredients with

4 eggs
1 tablespoon salt   1 cup catsup
⅛ teaspoon pepper   4 teaspoons lemon juice
2 teaspoons marjoram   2 teaspoons Worcestershire sauce
2 teaspoons basil   ⅔ cup milk
2 teaspoons thyme   1 teaspoon ground cloves

Mix well, but lightly. Fill ring molds and freeze. To serve, defrost, cover with aluminum foil and bake 2 hours at 350° with ring set in pan of water.

Unmold and serve with center filled with

Mashed potatoes
      or
Green vegetable

TUESDAY
TOMATO JUICE
* CASSOULET
MIXED SALAD
BLUEBERRY PIE (p. 128)

CASSOULET
(10 servings)

Soak overnight

3 cups Great Northern (marrow) beans

Put them in tightly covered pot with

2½ pounds lamb diced	1 bay leaf
9 frankfurters, thickly sliced	3 scallions, sliced
4 slices bacon	2 cloves garlic
3 tomatoes, peeled or 2-pound can tomatoes	1 teaspoon sugar
	1 teaspoon salt
¼ teaspoon thyme	¼ teaspoon pepper
¼ teaspoon marjoram	4 cups water

Bring to a boil, reduce heat and simmer for 2 hours. Chill quickly and freeze in portions suitable for your family. To serve, defrost and heat slowly for 30 minutes. Add water if necessary.

WEDNESDAY
* CHEDDAR CHEESE SOUP
* BAKED CHICKEN CASSEROLE
LIMAS IN CREAM (p. 56)
APPLESAUCE (p. 126)

CHEDDAR CHEESE SOUP
(12 servings)

Simmer in covered kettle until vegetables are tender, about 10 minutes

4½ cups diced potato
3 cups chopped onion

3 cups water

Puree vegetables and blend in

6 cups consommé
¾ pound grated Cheddar cheese

1½ cups cream

Freeze in suitable portions for your family. Defrost and heat to serve.

BAKED CHICKEN CASSEROLE
(12 servings)

Combine

3 cups catsup
1½ cups dry white wine
1 bunch parsley, chopped

3 cloves garlic, crushed
¾ teaspoon basil
9 sprigs rosemary

Pour this sauce over

3 3- to 3½-pound broilers, quartered

Freeze in portions suitable for your family. To serve, defrost and bake at 325°, basting, for about 1½ hours, until done.

THURSDAY
* Ham Stroganoff
Frozen String Beans
Honeybuns (p. 214)
Ice Cream

HAM STROGANOFF
(16 servings)

Cook according to package directions

3 8-ounce packages noodles

Drain and set aside.

Melt

　1 cup butter or margarine

In it sauté until tender

　2 cups finely chopped onion
　4 cloves garlic, finely chopped

　4 6-ounce cans sliced mushrooms, drained

Remove and discard gelatin and excess fat, and dice

　1 4-pound fully cooked canned ham

Add to onion mixture; heat, stirring, 5 minutes longer. Take from heat and stir in

　6 tablespoons flour
　4 8-ounce cans tomato sauce
　1 cup red Burgundy wine

　4 10½-ounce cans condensed beef bouillon
　1 teaspoon pepper

Simmer 10 minutes, stirring occasionally. Remove from heat; stir in

　4 cups sour cream

Divide into suitable portions for your use and place in greased casseroles in following manner: layer one-third of noodles; top with one-third of ham mixture; repeat layering twice. Freeze. To serve, defrost and sprinkle with

　1 cup Parmesan cheese per 8 servings

Bake, uncovered at 375° for 25 minutes.

FRIDAY

* CHICKEN OF THE SEA
BROAD EGG NOODLES
FROZEN BROCCOLI
POPOVERS (p. 215)
STEWED FRUIT (p. 132)

CHICKEN OF THE SEA
(12 servings)

Sauté

¾ pound mushrooms

½ cup butter

Drain and flake

  6 cans white-meat tuna

Place in casserole(s). Add

  Mushrooms
  3 cans cream of mushroom soup,
    diluted with
  1½ cups dry sherry

Sprinkle with

  1½ cups grated Parmesan cheese

Freeze in portions suitable for your family. To serve, defrost and bake at 350° for 45 minutes.

Mechanics and Timetable
for Cooking a Week at a Time

Here are a few of the mechanics for "cooking a week at a time" so that your freezer can reach that wonderful condition of being full of all the right things.

Whether you are a weekend or a nighttime cook, if you can spend just two hours at a time in the kitchen, you can make at least three of the main dishes from the preceding menus in whatever quantities you desire.

Do your shopping a day or two before and for your first venture try: Ham Loaf Van Allen (p. 30), Pot Roast (p. 31) and Polish Pork Chops (p. 39).

Your next KP might include Orange-Glazed Chicken (p. 38), Lamb Chops in Sour Cream (p. 41) and Hungarian Goulash (p. 36).

Or for economy you can devote the two hours to three dishes that utilize a sale-priced ingredient such as ground chuck.

You may find you can make more than three casseroles in two hours or you may have more than two hours, so you must work out your own plans. It will take you anywhere from a few weeks to a few months to collect the main dishes, soups and desserts suggested, but after that, cooking once a week for your family will do the trick. Cooking for parties and holidays takes additional time and we shall go into it in a future section of this book.

You will note that we do not suggest a casserole every single night. Just as people tire of lamb chops and roasts as a steady diet, combination dishes can jade the palate. We have suggested at least one plain main dish each week, but your family may want "un-adorned" food more often. So do what you wish with the menu plans. They are, after all, no more than suggestions.

As for the timing on any given menu—to allow you unharried dinner preparation, you might schedule the hours between 5 and 6 like this:

Week III, Tuesday Menu (p. 39)

Before you leave for work, remove the Picadillo from the freezer and allow to defrost.

5:00 Make your salad. Cover and refrigerate.
     Defrost the desired amount of pound cake and slice.
     Any small cookies will also defrost quickly.

5:15 Set the table.
     Read the paper!

5:30 Put the Picadillo on to cook.
     Back to the paper.

5:45 Put on the spaghetti.

5:55 Warm the Italian bread.
     Put the salad and dressing on the table.

6:00 Bring on the Picadillo, drained spaghetti and Italian bread.
     Ring the dinner bell and eat. You don't have to get up for any pot-watching. You need only clear the dishes and bring on the dessert.
     If you have coffee, either use an electric coffee maker, or put it on when you sit down to dinner and leave pot on asbestos pad over low heat. It will stay hot without boiling.

As you come to use the other menus you will find that they require no more work than this one. Not only will your family enjoy the restful surroundings at dinner but so will your stomach!

Lunch Making

Lunch making for the working gals usually means sandwiches or sandwiches and soups. Hot soup will stay hot in a thermos and sandwiches are a natural for assembly-line preparation. Once the filling is made, it is as easy to line up 24 slices of bread as six. Freeze for no more than two weeks in quantities suitable to your needs. Wrap individually and place frozen in lunch box. A sandwich will defrost in two to three hours and will be quite fresh at lunchtime.

Sandwich Fillings

Most fillings freeze quite successfully, but the "don'ts" from page 12 apply here with a few exceptions.

Mayonnaise may be used in a filling if it constitutes no more than one-third the volume.

Jelly does not freeze well.

Spread the bread to the edges with butter or margarine to prevent the fillings from making it soggy.

Here are a few suggestions for fillings:

Ham loaf
Meat loaf
Cheese
Roast beef
Cold cuts
Chicken
Turkey
Peanut butter and bacon
Cheese and olives
Ham
Tuna fish salad
Ground beef and catsup
Corned beef and India relish
Cream cheese and dried beef

Shrimp and chutney, etc., etc.

See also the fillings under tea sandwiches, pp. 191-193.

Ready? Set? Run, do not walk, to your nearest grocery store and start buying!

GILDING THE FROZEN LILY

Utilizing Commercially Frozen Foods

Although we know one lady who is a holdout and uses only fresh vegetables and meats in her kitchen, we emphasize the fact that she is the only one we know! Commercially frozen foods are here to stay, and most of us are modern enough to admit it.

Day by day we are using more and more of the foods we find in the frozen food cases. The most successfully frozen foods in terms of taste, texture and appearance are the vegetables. They are, of course, far closer to fresh tasting than their canned relatives and are as readily available year round.

If you have the time and inclination to shell peas or french string beans and are able to get them fresh from the farm—by all means go ahead! (And if you are really ambitious and freeze them when in season, you *are* ahead of the game!) Nothing can equal the fresh product, but the vegetables found in today's supermarket have been traveling so long that there is very little that is fresh about them by the time they reach your pot.

We can heartily endorse almost all frozen uncooked vegetables, with a few exceptions—one of which is corn on the cob. But then we consider corn more than a half hour old not worth eating. As a result we devour it during July, August and September and dream about it the other nine months.

Frozen vegetables should not be defrosted before cooking and the following is a very nutritious and delicious method for cooking them. Place the vegetables in a heavy pot with *no water*, 1 tablespoon butter (optional) and salt. Cook them, covered, very slowly, and the liquid from the vegetables themselves is sufficient to keep them from burning. They will not only taste marvelous, but will

have kept a goodly amount of their vitamins. Though they take longer to cook—asparagus, for example, requires 20 minutes—you don't have to baby-sit with them.

You may also want to cook your frozen vegetables in the oven. Since no water is used, this is extremely nutritious.

Place frozen vegetables in greased casserole. Top with 1 to 2 tablespoons butter or margarine * and ½ teaspoon salt. Cover and bake from 50 to 65 minutes at 325°. At 350° deduct 10 minutes baking time.† Stir 15 minutes before cooking is completed.

To grill frozen vegetables when cooking outdoors, let the vegetables stand at room temperature for three hours. Place vegetables on a 12-inch square of heavy-duty aluminum foil. For seasoning place 1 pat of butter under and one on top of vegetables. ‡ Sprinkle with salt. Cover with 12-inch square foil. Roll edges together to make tight seal, but allow room for steam.

Lay package on rack 2½ inches from heat.

Cook from 30 to 50 minutes. Turn package when halfway cooked.

If you want to dress up your vegetables, many delicious recipes can be adapted to a package or two of the frozen varieties. Recipe suggestions will be found later in the chapter.

In order to save time during the actual cooking of some of the vegetable recipes, you might assemble, chop, slice, etc., everything but the frozen foods the day before. At serving time, simply combine and cook.

Certain fried frozen vegetables can be made quite delicious by cooking them in fat rather than baking them in the oven. They will be much crisper and more nearly resemble the freshly made products. This actually applies to all frozen fried foods such as fish sticks, fried shrimp and clams, hush puppies, etc. It is especially recommended for cooking the frozen varieties of french fries, french-fried onion rings and fried eggplant.   P.S. Shoestring french fries are the crispest of all frozen french fries.

---

* Add 2 tablespoons water to lima beans.
  Add 2 tablespoons milk to cauliflower.
† Asparagus spears take 70 minutes at 325°.
‡ Sprinkle limas and mixed vegetables with 2 tablespoons water; sprinkle cauliflower with 1 tablespoon lemon juice.

ARTICHOKES AND MUSHROOMS
(8 servings)

In

¼ pound butter

Sauté

3 1-pound packages of frozen artichokes, lightly sprinkled with lemon

1 pound fresh mushrooms, sliced
4 tablespoons grated onion

Season with

Salt and pepper

Serve immediately.

BAKED ASPARAGUS
(8 servings)

Cook according to directions on page 50

2 packages frozen asparagus

In skillet heat until brown

½ cup butter
Salt

Paprika

Toss with

1 cup bread crumbs

Alternate layers in greased casserole of

Asparagus   Bread crumbs

You may refrigerate at this point. To serve, bake at 325° for 20 to 25 minutes.

CAULIFLOWER WITH BLACK OLIVES
(6 servings)

Cook according to directions on page 50

   2 packages frozen cauliflower

Combine and heat, but do not boil

   1 egg, beaten   ½ teaspoon salt
   ½ cup sour cream   ¼ teaspoon paprika
   2 tablespoons lemon juice

Add

   ½ cup pitted ripe olives, sliced

Pour over hot drained cauliflower.

CORN PUDDING
(Serves 4)

Cook as directed on page 50

   1 package frozen corn niblets

Combine cooked corn with

   1 tablespoon butter   1 teaspoon salt
   ¼ cup sugar   ¾ cup milk
   1 egg, beaten

Bake at 450° for 30 minutes, until top is browned.

DOUBLE DREAM POTATOES
(Serve 4)

Melt

   2 tablespoons butter or margarine

Add

   ¾ cup chopped onion
   2 9-ounce packages frozen french fried potatoes

Panfry, stirring constantly until potatoes are hot.

Remove from heat and add

>1 cup shredded Cheddar cheese   1¼ teaspoons salt
>¾ cup ready-to-eat whole bran   ⅛ teaspoon pepper
> cereal, crushed

Mix well and pour into shallow 1½-quart casserole.

Beat

>½ pint sour cream   2 eggs

Pour over casserole. Bake at 350° for about 15 minutes.

FRENCH-FRIED ONIONS AND GREEN BEANS
(8 servings)

Place in 2 9-inch or equivalent baking dishes

>2 pounds frozen green beans   1 can water chestnuts, sliced and
>2 10½-ounce cans mushroom soup   drained
>½ teaspoon oregano

Bake at 350° for 25 minutes.

Top with

>2 3½-ounce cans french-fried onion rings

Bake 5 minutes more.

GREEN BEANS CHILI
(8 servings)

Brown, drain and crumble

>2 slices bacon

Combine with

>½ cup chili sauce   1 teaspoon brown sugar
>¼ cup finely chopped onion   ½ teaspoon dry mustard
>1 teaspoon salt

Refrigerate if desired. To serve, combine with

>2 pounds frozen green beans

Place ingredients in 1½-quart greased casserole. Cover and bake at 350°
for 40 minutes. Stir once or twice.

GREEN PEA SALAD
(Serves 8)

Cook according to directions on page 50 until just heated through, using ¼ *cup water*

   3 10-ounce packages frozen peas

Drain and reserve ¼ cup cooking liquid.

To liquid add

⅓ cup salad oil   ¾ teaspoon salt
2⅔ tablespoons red wine vinegar   1 tablespoon minced fresh mint

Pour over peas, cover and chill at least 6 hours.

Just before serving stir in

½ cup finely diced celery   ¼ cup sour cream

Serve in large lettuce-lined salad bowl.

Border with

   Tomato wedges

LIMAS IN CREAM
(8 servings)

Cook according to directions on page 50

   2 packages frozen limas

Sauté

2 tablespoons minced onion   2 tablespoons butter

Add limas along with

1 teaspoon marjoram   ½ cup light cream
½ chopped pimento   Salt and pepper

Refrigerate if desired. To serve, heat thoroughly.

PARTY SQUASH
(6 servings)

Thaw in greased casserole for 4 hours

   2 packages frozen cooked squash

Stir in

2 tablespoons melted butter
¼ cup chopped pecans
¼ cup thin honey

2 teaspoons salt
¼ teaspoon nutmeg

Sprinkle top with

¼ cup chopped pecans

Dot with

1 tablespoon butter

Bake at 350° for 20 to 30 minutes.

PEAS SUPRÊME
(6 servings)

Place in lightly greased casserole

2 packages frozen peas
2 3-ounce cans mushrooms, drained

3 tablespoons butter
2 tablespoons diced pimientos

Cover tightly and bake at 400° for 30 minutes.

POTATO PUFFS PARMESAN

Bake 15 to 20 minutes according to package directions

Frozen potato puffs

Sprinkle generously with

Grated Parmesan cheese

Run under broiler for 2 to 3 minutes.
Excellent with meat or as hors d'oeuvres.

POTATO STIX PARMESAN
(6 servings)

Arrange in single layer in shallow pan

2 packages frozen french fries

Brush with

¼ cup melted butter

Sprinkle with

  1 teaspoon onion salt   Paprika

Bake at 425° for 25 minutes. Remove from pan and sprinkle with

  ½ cup grated Parmesan cheese

Shake to coat evenly. Serve immediately.

SPINACH BALLS
(8 servings)

Combine and mix well

  2 packages frozen chopped   2 tablespoons grated Parmesan
      spinach, cooked and drained,   cheese
      page 50   1 egg
  1 cup bread crumbs   ⅛ teaspoon allspice
  2 tablespoons grated onion   1 teaspoon salt

Let stand 15 minutes. Shape into 1-inch balls. Combine

  1 egg   ¼ cup cold water

Roll balls in

  Bread crumbs

then in egg mixture, then in crumbs again.

Freeze. To serve, defrost and fry in 1 inch fat for 5 minutes.

WALNUT BROCCOLI
(8 servings)

Cook until barely tender, according to directions on page 50

  3 packages frozen chopped broccoli

Drain and place in buttered casserole. In small pan melt

  ½ cup butter

Take from heat and blend in

  4 tablespoons flour
  1½ tablespoons powdered chicken-
      stock base

Gradually add

  2 cups milk

Return to heat and cook, stirring until smooth and boiling. Pour over broccoli. Heat together

  ⅔ cup water   **6** tablespoons butter

When butter melts add

  ⅔ package herb-stuffing mix   **⅔** cup chopped walnuts

Top broccoli with stuffing mixture. Refrigerate if desired. To serve, bake at 400° for 20 to 30 minutes.

Commercially frozen fruits, especially with a few ice crystals still in them, are delicious, with the exception of melon balls which lose all their crispness in freezing. There are now available some flash frozen "dry pack" fruits such as strawberries and blueberries, and if you have not been foresighted enough to "freeze-it-yourself" (nothing could be easier) these are excellent substitutes when the fresh fruits are out of season.

Most of the frozen fruit juices are of good taste and high quality.

You can defrost frozen fruits in 20 minutes, simply by placing the unopened container under running cold water.

BELGIAN WAFFLES
(From the New York World's Fair, 1964-65)

Top

  2 warm frozen or freshly made waffles

with

  Whipped cream

and

  Frozen, sliced, sweetened strawberries (defrosted)

CHERRY SUNDAE

Separate the juice from

  1 20-ounce can cherries

Stir a little juice into

   1 tablespoon cornstarch

Stir it back into the remaining juice over low heat until thickened and clear. Pour while still warm over cherries. Then pour the cherries and their sauce over vanilla ice cream.

FROZEN FRUITS AND LIQUEUR

Sprinkle partially defrosted fruits with

   Kirsch, brandy, sherry or sweet wine

FROZEN FRUITS CHANTILLY
(6 servings)

Red raspberries, blueberries, peaches, strawberries (any combination).
Combine

   1 quart defrosted fruit—drained

with

   1 cup heavy cream, whipped *
   Few drops vanilla

Chill 2 hours or longer and serve in parfait glasses.

FROZEN STRAWBERRIES ROMANOFF
(6 servings)

Combine

   ½ cup orange juice   ½ cup curaçao

Pour over partially defrosted

   Strawberries †

Chill at least 1 hour. At serving time, heap berries in serving dish and
garnish with

   1 cup heavy cream, whipped and flavored with confectioners' sugar
   to taste

   Additional curaçao

   * If fruits are unsweetened, sweeten whipped cream slightly with powdered sugar.
   † If strawberries are unsweetened, combine them with ⅓ cup sugar.

PEACHY-ORANGE SAUCE

Combine in saucepan

1 package frozen peach slices ⅛ teaspoon cinnamon
½ 6-ounce can frozen orange juice ⅛ teaspoon salt
concentrate

Bring to boil, lower heat and simmer for 15 minutes. Cool slightly before spooning over

Ice cream

After leaving the fruit and vegetable departments, we come to a fairly new product that is coming into its own—the frozen bread and biscuit or roll doughs. With these doughs you can have the fragrance of home baked products without any of the time-consuming preparation.

When using the frozen bread dough, begin by following the directions on the package about thawing and allowing the dough to rise. Then the dough is ready to shape in one of the ways shown here or in some special way that you invent yourself.

STREUSEL COFFEE CAKE

Prepare the dough as directed on package. Divide into two pieces

1 loaf of frozen bread dough

Press each piece into a well-buttered square or round cake pan. Combine until crumbly

¼ cup flour 1 teaspoon cinnamon
¼ cup sugar ¼ cup chopped nuts
1 tablespoon melted butter

Sprinkle this mixture over top of dough. Cover; let rise in warm draft-free place until doubled in bulk. Bake at 375° 25 to 35 minutes. Serve warm.

FROSTED TEA RING

Prepare as directed on package

  1 loaf dough

Roll into a rectangle 9 by 18 inches. Spread with

  2 tablespoons softened butter

Sprinkle with a mixture of

  2 teaspoons cinnamon   ½ cup raisins
  ½ cup sugar

Roll into long tight roll and seal ends together to form a ring. Place on a greased cookie sheet. Cut slashes at one-inch intervals and fan out edges. Let rise in warm, draft-free place until double in bulk. Bake at 375° about 25 to 35 minutes. Remove from baking sheet and if desired drizzle while still hot with

  Confectioners' sugar mixed with a little water to make thin icing

Decorate if desired with

  Nuts   Candied fruits

BREAD STICKS

Prepare as directed on package

  1 loaf dough

Pinch off small pieces of dough. Roll out on board with palm of hand to form very thin rolls about 8 inches long. Place on greased cookie sheet. Brush with a mixture of

  1 egg white   2 tablespoons water

Sprinkle with

  Coarse salt, sesame or caraway seeds

Let rise, uncovered, for about 30 minutes. Bake at 425° for 10 minutes or until golden brown.

ORANGE-RAISIN SHORTCAKE
(Makes 12)

Bake according to package directions

> 1 package (1 dozen) frozen biscuits

Defrost

> 1 6-ounce can frozen orange-juice concentrate

just enough to remove from can; place in saucepan with

> 1 cup raisins

Combine

> 1 cup brown sugar   ½ teaspoon ground cloves
> 2 tablespoons flour

Mix with

> ¼ cup butter or margarine, softened

Stir sugar mixture into orange juice and cook, stirring, until thickened, about 5 minutes. Serve hot on hot biscuits. Sauce may be stored in refrigerator and reheated.

One of the wonders of the freezing world is the dough from which the excellent but exceedingly difficult-to-make baklava and strudel is made.

It takes much practice, short fingernails and unlimited patience to fashion holeless dough.

Now it is possible to make all of these pastries, main dishes and hors d'oeuvres with frozen leaves, available at many specialty grocers.

It is still important to work carefully and quickly but after one attempt you can achieve perfect results. We have included two Middle Eastern recipes utilizing the leaves; you will find additional ones on the box itself.

CHEESE BOEREG

These are super hors d'oeuvres that are usually consumed as fast as they make their appearance.

Defrost completely (overnight in refrigerator)

   1 box phyllo leaves or strudel dough

Remove sheets from the box and cut into three sections lengthwise. Keep the sections covered with a damp cloth and place on a damp towel. It is necessary to work quickly so that the dough will not dry out and become brittle.

Fold over about 1½ inches at the bottom of a single strip and spread the strip with

   Melted butter

Using about

   1 teaspoon of filling

place the filling at the folded end. Fold up to make a triangular shape.

Fold as you fold the American flag. When the strip is completely folded its shape is that of a triangle. Place all the little triangles on a cookie sheet and brush with

   Melted butter

Bake at 300° 12 to 15 minutes or until delicately golden brown. Freeze. To serve, reheat, frozen, at 300° for 3 to 5 minutes.

Filling:

Combine thoroughly

½ pound grated Münster cheese	1 finely minced clove garlic
10 to 12 ounces creamed cottage cheese	1½ tablespoons finely chopped parsley
2 eggs	Salt to taste
1 very small onion, grated	

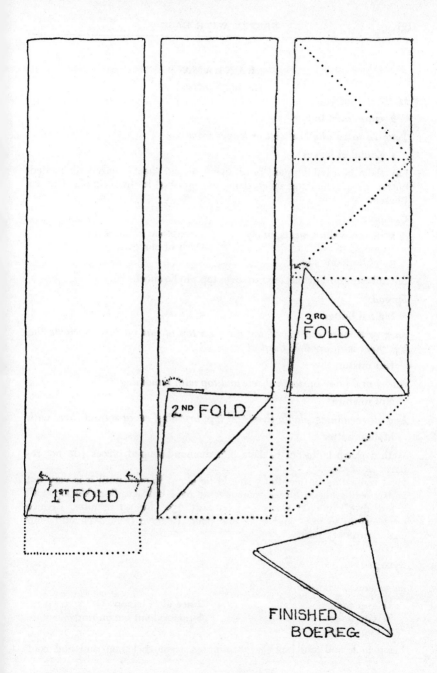

BAKLAVA
(30 to 36 pieces)

Melt

2 cups sweet butter

Take 10 to 12 phyllo sheets or leaves from

1 pound of leaves

Lay them in a baking pan; brush every second sheet evenly with melted butter. Keep remaining sheets damp as described in the recipe for Cheese Boereg.

Combine

1 pound walnut meats, finely chopped	1 teaspoon cinnamon
5 tablespoons sugar	Dash of cloves

Spread one-third of this mixture over top phyllo sheet.

Spread

Melted butter

on 5 or 6 more sheets and lay them on top of nut mixture. Sprinkle the top sheet with another third of

Nut mixture

Add 5 or 6 more buttered sheets and top with remaining

Nut mixture

Lay all remaining phyllo sheets on top, brushing every second sheet with

Melted butter

With a sharp knife cut baklava into diamond-shaped pieces (do not remove from pan).

Heat remaining butter—there should be about ½ cup—until it is very hot and is beginning to brown; pour evenly over baklava. Sprinkle top with a few drops of cold water and bake at 350° for 30 minutes. Reduce temperature to 300° and bake one hour. Remove from oven and pour cool syrup over pastry.

Syrup:

In saucepan combine

¾ cup sugar	Juice of ½ lemon
¾ cup honey	Squeezed-out lemon rind
2 cups water	

Bring to a boil and boil for 20 minutes. Remove lemon rind and cool.

TYDINGS TORTE
(Serves 10)

Cut into seven layers,

1 frozen pound cake

Melt over hot water

1 6-ounce package chocolate chips

Remove from heat and add

1 teaspoon instant coffee   1 cup sour cream

Frost each of the layers and frost the entire cake. This will keep three weeks in the refrigerator!

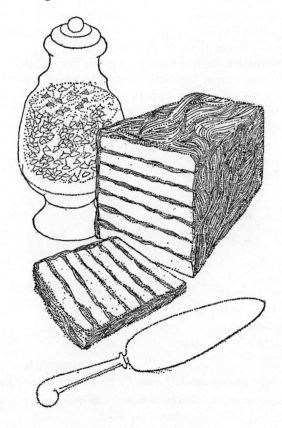

The frozen puff pastry shells are really incomparable and no longer worth the trouble to make at home. To stretch leftover chicken à la king, curry, lobster Newburg, etc., fill the hot baked shells with hot food. This dish, so easy to prepare, looks surprisingly elegant.

Keep the shells on hand for festive ice cream dishes, too. Spoon some chocolate sauce, stewed raspberries, etc., over the ice-cream filled shells.

Besides ice cream, the only commercially frozen dessert better than the one you struggle with at home is the puff pastry turnover and it is the only dessert we don't think you should doctor.

The frozen unbaked pie shells are quite good too and will always do in an emergency.

Many other commercially frozen foods are quite tasty, but many more are an insult to the palate, so use them with discretion and do not hesitate to doctor them when necessary.

Many of the frozen soups are very good. For a delightful luncheon or elegant supper-in-a-hurry, serve frozen Welsh rarebit on frozen spinach soufflé. (Do cook it!) With a salad and frozen biscuits, the supper is complete.

Frozen tortillas are a boon to Mexican food lovers.

SEA FOOD. Many of the frozen shellfish are quite good; they seem to freeze commercially far more successfully than poultry or meat. We have included three recipes utilizing seafood below.

CAULIFLOWER–SHRIMP DISH
(Serves 8)

Melt

   6 tablespoons butter

Take from heat, stir in

   4 tablespoons flour

Gradually add

   2 cups milk   Salt and pepper to taste

Stir over medium heat until thickened. On bottom of casserole place

   2 packages frozen cauliflower, sufficiently defrosted to separate pieces

Top with

  2 pounds frozen shrimp

Pour the cream sauce over this. Top with

  1 cup grated Cheddar cheese (optional)
  1 cup toasted slivered almonds

Bake at 350° for 40 minutes.

ROCK LOBSTER TAILS AU BEURRE
(6 Servings)

Brush

  6 frozen rock lobster tails

with

  ¼ cup melted butter

Sprinkle with

  Garlic salt

Grill shell side down 15 minutes. Turn and grill 15 minutes more. Serve with following sauce.

Lemon Butter Sauce:

Heat together

  ½ cup butter   1 teaspoon salt
  2 tablespoons lemon juice   Dash cayenne pepper

TEMPURA
JAPANESE-STYLE FRIED SHRIMP

Fry according to package directions

  1 package frozen breaded butterfly shrimp

Serve them with

  Soy sauce
  Hot mustard (made with dry mustard mixed with beer)

For the most part, commercially frozen foods are a great improvement over their canned counterparts, and when used judiciously they can save many hours in the kitchen. When it comes to prepared dishes, however, the homemade product can rarely be duplicated.

FEASIBLE FREEZABLES

From Soup to Nuts

We had more fun researching this section than any other. In addition to the meats, fruits and vegetables which we had long since found freezable, there were so many surprising discoveries to be made!

DAIRY PRODUCTS. We never really knew what to do with extra egg yolks if we weren't inspired to bake that very day, so into a small container they would go, waiting to be remembered for someone's scrambled eggs. Somehow the little container always got lost in the back corner of the refrigerator, only to be discovered when the yolks were beyond help!

EGGS. Don't forget the rest of the egg. Freeze them whole or separated. Freeze *whole eggs* in ice cube trays. Select as many eggs as there are sections, break in a bowl and stir just enough to mix. Add either ¾ teaspoon sugar or ¼ teaspoon salt per ½ cup (about 6 eggs). Put eggs in tray. Set divider in place. When frozen, the cubes may be put in plastic bags, each cube equaling one egg.

When freezing *yolks* only, add either ¾ teaspoon sugar or ¼ teaspoon salt per ½ cup of yolks. Use the former in cakes, the latter in hollandaise, etc. Freeze in rigid containers in quantities of 4, 5 or 6, which will usually fill most recipe requirements. One tablespoon yolk equals one egg yolk. Mark the container with quantity of yolks and designate "salt" or "sugar."

Freeze *whites*, as is, marking containers as to quantity. 2 tablespoons white equal one egg white.

Defrost eggs overnight in refrigerator.

Ground hard-cooked egg whites can be frozen and used for garnish.

CHEESE. Most freeze well. Pasteurized processed, Roquefort and Bleu will crumble more easily when frozen. Parmesan and Romano grate quite readily; Cheddar shreds quickly. Cream cheese becomes crumbly but not in combination with other foods. If after defrosting a cream cheese dip seems grainy, whip it well. Brick, Port-Salut, Swiss, Provolone, Mozzarella, Liederkranz and Camembert all freeze well.

MILK, CREAM AND BUTTER. Milk may be frozen for emergencies. Shake well after defrosting. Cream can be frozen and heavy cream whips quite readily if a few ice crystals remain. Freeze in original cartons if there is ½-inch headroom.

You may find it handy to cut butter into fancy shapes for parties and freeze until needed. When freezing butter in original container, overwrap it; butter is very susceptible to other odors.

SAUCES. Freeze cream sauce, béchamel, béarnaise, hollandaise, Mornay, brown and white wine sauces. With béarnaise or hollandaise reheat by stirring in top of double boiler. Begin with two tablespoons, add two more, etc., stirring between each addition. Stir all sauces as you reheat to prevent separation. To prevent scorching use top of double boiler. Defrost before reheating. Sauces frozen in cubes are handy when only one or two servings of vegetables or meat are being prepared.

STOCKS. *All stocks*—fish, meat, chicken, etc., freeze perfectly.

BAKED GOODS. Refrigerator biscuits, those that come in cans, can be frozen if partially baked. Defrost and finish baking. Follow package directions for temperature.

Freeze English muffins. While frozen, slice in half. Butter and broil 4 inches from heat.

Freeze plain, cinnamon and jelly doughnuts up to 1 month. Heat at 400° to serve.

Freeze bread crumbs, buttered or plain. Make your own when you find yourself with a large crust collection. A blender makes lovely crumbs.

Both lemon meringue pies (without meringue) and cooked chiffon pies (if made either with whipped cream or egg whites) will freeze up to a month.

FISH. Shellfish are quite freezable. Wash, shuck and wash again clams, oysters and scallops (usually already shucked). Freeze them in their own liquor.

Freeze crabs and lobsters cooked and shelled.

Freeze shrimp raw, shelled and deveined. They may be frozen after cooking but they tend to toughen when defrosted if not in combination with other ingredients.

HERBS. Chop and freeze fresh herbs such as mint, dill, parsley, rosemary, etc. Some of them do not look too attractive when defrosted, but their flavor has it all over the dried varieties (which aren't much to look at either!). You might find it handy to make bouquets garnis. Tie together in cheesecloth an assortment of fresh

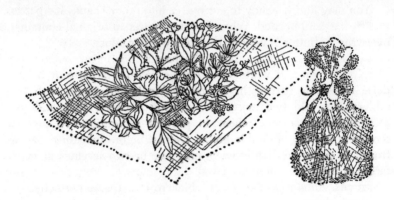

herbs, usually including parsley, thyme and bay leaf and sometimes fennel, leek, marjoram and tarragon. The bouquet can then be removed from the pot easily. Use without defrosting.

SWEETS. Freeze popcorn, candy bars, marshmallows. Cut marshmallows while frozen. No sticking problems. Citron and glacéed fruits retain their moisture and freshness. Stock up at Christmas. It is often difficult to buy them at any other time.

Some frostings freeze well—butter, confectioners' sugar and fudge. Remember that boiled frostings get sticky.

Brown sugar will not harden or lump if frozen.

You may freeze mousses and steamed puddings.

NUTS. Freeze nutmeats, whole, chopped, slivered or buttered and toasted.

FATS. Freeze suet and salt pork in small quantities.

ICE CUBES. You can save yourself 50¢ or $1.00 plus a last-minute trip before a party by freezing your own ice cubes in quantity. Empty frozen cubes into plastic bags for accessibility at any time and especially for parties. You might want to freeze cubes with a cherry, olive or cocktail onion in the center for drinks.

Have we surprised and delighted you? Further "eye-opener" conveniences are coming in the next chapter.

Do-It-Yourself TV Dinners

Leftovers

One day a few years ago we stopped to visit a friend who was busy in the kitchen. Although we had been recipe-swapping for several years we were stunned to see her portioning out bits of meat, potato and vegetable into sectioned aluminum plates. What in heaven's name? From leftovers, our friend was making her own TV dinners, which her family vastly preferred to the commercial product. Since that momentous day we, too, have found how inexpensive and tasty they are. And how handy for leaving with the baby-sitter when Daddy decides to take Mommy out for dinner.

That explains the title of this chapter, but by no means tells the whole story of your freezer, your leftovers and you.

Leftovers have gone the way of the old gray mare. If treated with care and handled with imagination, they can provide not only family sustenance, but may even be elegant enough to provide the basis for a party dish. It is really surprising how many classic dishes can be created with leftovers. The secret is in the sauce, the touch of ingenuity and that precious package of leftovers carefully tucked away in the freezer for just such an opportunity.

Keep in mind the foods mentioned in the preceding section as they often belong in the leftover class. Those egg yolks and whites can be the beginnings of something as elegant as hollandaise sauce or florentines (p. 117).

In many instances, it is necessary to accumulate a few scraps at a time until you have enough to be of any use.

If baby eats only 1 tablespoonful of baby food at a meal, the jar could last forever! So use the jar for two days and freeze it. Two weeks later baby might like the contents better and might eat more. One of the baby food companies even puts out a recipe book to help you utilize the contents of the little jars. If you collect enough, they can be useful for adult fare: strained peas in pea soup, strained spinach in spinach tarte, mashed bananas in banana cake; see page 170 for use of baby food carrots.

Coffee and tea may be frozen in ice cube trays. When frozen transfer to plastic bags. Use instead of regular cubes for iced tea or coffee. The drinks will not dilute as the cubes melt.

Cut stale bread into tiny cubes; toast them dry or brushed with melted butter for croutons to freeze and serve with soups. Sprinkle with garlic or celery salt if desired.

Too many pancakes, French toast or waffles? Freeze. Toast in toaster or 375° oven to serve.

As you collect pastry scraps place them in a plastic bag. When you have gathered enough you have a free crust!

Freeze unconsumed sandwiches and, for an extra treat, brush with melted butter and toast.

Partially used cans and jars of pickles, pimientos and olives freeze well in their own liquor. When you are lucky enough to find fresh ginger buy it and freeze it. When needed, grate the frozen piece, return unused portion to freezer.

Leftover whipped cream may be frozen. If you are really ambitious, squeeze it out through a decorating tube onto a cookie sheet, or drop by tablespoons. Flash freeze and remove to plastic bag. To defrost, remove from bag; 30 minutes at room temperature is all that is needed, or serve a frozen rosette of cream on a hot pudding.

Ice cream, after it has been opened, should be overwrapped to prevent formation of ice crystals.

Leftover grated lemon, orange and lime peel should be frozen in plastic containers. Keep adding or use as needed.

Unused lemon and lime juice can be frozen in individual ice cube sections. Measure and mark quantities. Remove cubes to plastic bags and use as needed.

Syrup from canned fruits may be frozen into cubes and used for cold drinks in the summertime or hot fruit sauce for a dessert.

Opened packages of prunes, raisins, dates, figs and grated coconut will maintain their freshness if frozen.

Crumble those extra pieces of cooked bacon and freeze. Use as topping for baked potatoes or combine with peanut butter for sandwich spread.

Small amounts of cooked ham may be chopped or ground and frozen until you have enough for stuffing mushrooms, making casseroles or waffles, etc.

Ham bones, steak bones, etc.—collect them for soup.

Chicken necks, gizzards, hearts and their relations will freeze long enough to collect in sufficient quantity for "free" chicken soup.

What can you do with cold leftover baked potatoes? As each one comes along, cut it in half, scoop out and mash. Combine with salt and pepper, sour cream and chives or grated Cheddar cheese. Replace in shells. Freeze. They are lovely for company when baked at 350° for 20 to 30 minutes after defrosting.

Partially used cans and jars of water chestnuts, bamboo shoots and ready-to-use sauerkraut freeze well in their own liquor.

Chop the whole green pepper or onion even if only part is needed. Freeze the rest in plastic containers. Keep adding or use as needed.

The cooked vegetables and meats that do not go into the "TV dinners" are good for soups.

And speaking of those dinners, be sure to cover sliced cooked meat or poultry with its own gravy, fried foods excepted. For the starchy vegetable, cooked rice may be used in place of potato. To serve the dinner bake 30 to 45 minutes at 375°. Remove the foil from fried foods after the first 20 minutes.

If your leftover meat doesn't have gravy you might try these sauces to freeze and serve with the meat.

BARBECUE L.O.
(4 servings)

Brown

1 large onion, chopped   4 tablespoons butter

Add

2 8-ounce cans tomato sauce   2 teaspoons salt
1 cup catsup   2 teaspoons chili powder
4 tablespoons brown sugar   1 teaspoon celery salt
4 tablespoons vinegar   Dash tabasco
4 teaspoons Worcestershire
sauce

Simmer 15 minutes. Add

4 cups leftover meat, cut up or sliced.

Freeze. To serve, defrost and heat through.

LAMB CREOLE
(4 servings)

Beat well together

3 tablespoons olive oil   1½ tablespoons vinegar
2 tablespoons chili sauce   Dash salt, pepper, thyme, bay leaf
1½ tablespoons Worcestershire
sauce

Stir in

1 cup boiling beef stock (made with 2 bouillon cubes)

Mixed with

2 grated onions   1 large clove garlic, crushed

Cook for 15 minutes. Pour over

4 cups cooked lamb, cut up or sliced

Freeze. To serve, defrost and heat through.

ROAST BEEF IN CUMBERLAND SAUCE
(4 servings)

Over hot water stir

2 10-ounce jars currant jelly

until soft. Beat in

2 egg yolks	4 tablespoons sugar
½ cup raisins	1½ teaspoons dry mustard
4 tablespoons vinegar	Salt and pepper to taste

Stir the sauce, occasionally, until it thickens, about 15 minutes. Pour over

4 cups cold roast beef

If desired, return the beef and the sauce to the double boiler or freeze in sauce. To serve, defrost and reheat in double boiler.

SWEET-AND-SOUR TONGUE
(4 servings)

Cut into julienne strips

4 cups tongue

Place in baking dish. Mix together

½ cup brown sugar	1 tablespoon cornstarch

Combine with

1 cup tongue broth or beef stock

Add

½ teaspoon whole cloves	½ bay leaf

Cook, stirring, until thick. Add

1 cup drained, pitted sour cherries, frozen or canned	1 tablespoon lemon juice
	2 tablespoons butter or margarine

Bring to a boil. Pour over tongue and bake in 350° oven for 20 minutes. Freeze. To serve, defrost and reheat in double boiler.

By this time it should be self-evident that a prudent use of leftovers is a grand economy. In the past the leftovers entered the refrigerator, seldom to return to edible state. Whether we would forget them on purpose or not remains a moot point. Today with the freezer, the pressure is taken off! You can use as needed and —more important—as desired.

JUST BETWEEN YOU AND ME AND THE FREEZER

Hints

Although this section is not very long, it contains some of the most important information about frozen food preparation in the book. In many instances little hints can make the difference between a perfect result and one that loses something between the time it enters the freezer and enters your mouth!

It is exceedingly important to undercook prepared foods that must be reheated for serving. If they require a good deal of time to reheat, they may be undercooked by as much as ½ hour.

Be certain, also, to cool prepared dishes quickly, to stop the cooking process. Place the dish either in ice water or on ice cubes.

Skim off as much fat as possible from the surface of stews, soups, etc.; then freeze.

Trim fat from uncooked meat as well. It has a tendency to turn rancid over a long freezing period.

Changes of flavor in spices can take place. Salt and onions can decrease. Cloves, curry and garlic can change.

In the pie department we suggest that you freeze mince and pumpkin pies before baking. Many authorities would also include fruit pies in this category. Our experience has been that frozen baked fruit pies, properly reheated at serving time, will produce equally good results.

However, an unbaked fruit pie to be frozen should have its juice thickened with tapioca or cornstarch in place of the flour; one and one-half times the amount of the thickening agent that the recipe calls for.

Do not cut vents in any kind of covered pie before freezing. Make the cuts after the first 10 minutes of baking.

If you should find yourself in the mood to make pie crusts and only pie crusts, one day, we would suggest that you freeze them unbaked and unshaped. They take up almost no room this way. Make the crust as usual and roll it out 2 inches wider in diameter than the pie plate in which it is to fit. For an 11-inch pie plate your crust should be 13 inches in diameter. Place two sheets of aluminum foil between each pastry circle to facilitate separation. Place all the circles between two stiff pieces of cardboard to prevent cracking; wrap. To use, remove desired number. They will defrost in 20 to 30 minutes. When soft enough to shape, place in pie plate and flute as usual. Chill if necessary before baking. Baking time is the same as for unfrozen shells.

Many feel that the exception to the rule that nothing improves with freezing is lard pastry. Something in the freezing process makes for more tender pastries and flakier ones.

For all gooey or sticky foods such as whipped cream, frosted cakes, open-face canapés, etc., flash freeze them uncovered. As soon as they are frozen wrap as usual for freezing. To defrost, remove wrapping first.

Variations in baking time of defrosted foods are dependent upon the length of time the defrosted food has been at room temperature.

If a cheese dip seems grainy after defrosting, whip it well.

Making soup concentrates is a space-saving device. Prepare the soups as usual, but use a smaller amount of water. Omit milk. Freeze. To serve, add required amount of liquids and cook.

No doubt, if you are a longtime freezer owner you have dreamed up some of your own shortcuts and space savers. One good idea seems to beget another. The more we use our freezers the more wonderful things we find to use them for; and you are certain to feel that way about your own freezer after a few short months of having it around.

Once you have reached the point of having enough frozen meals to feed your family for a week you will want to move on to quantity cooking for all kinds of occasions. Our next chapter will spur you on.

3

The More the Merrier

The More the Merrier

QUANTITY COOKING FOR THE FREEZER

The working housewife is not the only one to benefit from a home freezer, nor is the hostess, for the rest of the family really reaps most of the pleasure without any of the work! Quite seriously, the freezer is a reliable friend to all homemakers day in and day out, but it should be treated with the proper attitude and respect. (Think of it as a venerable great-grandmother!) Certainly a freezer *is* grand for stockpiling bargains in uncooked meat, poultry and produce. However, it is even better as a convenience and economizer if it is used to stockpile cooked foods and the more the merrier. A rainy afternoon and an extra dozen eggs should provide enough inspiration to fill a few of those empty spaces in the freezer, but the thought of unexpected guests, the necessity for holiday baking and the desire to take advantage of abundant seasonal produce should really spur you on to quantity cooking.

One businesslike and efficient method for doing this is known as Chain Cooking. It has the further advantage of being great fun if done with a companion cook. Just plan extra carefully so that the adage about two women in the kitchen won't apply. It would be an awfully silly way to lose an old friend!

The threat of unexpected guests will drive us to the freezer every time. Though the kind of surprise company may vary, this subject is close to the hearts of most homemakers. Many wives today are inevitably called by their husbands at the zero hour and told, as casually as can be, that there will be one or two extra for dinner. One friend of ours has in-laws who prefer not to announce their visits in advance, feeling, they say, that this custom will cause less fuss and muss! (One doesn't argue with one's in-laws, however!)

In a city like Washington (home for one of us) everyone we've ever known comes through town at one time or another. Somehow the visitor always calls to say "Hello" at 5:00 P.M. (To be perfectly honest, we love it!) A well-stocked freezer will take care of all such situations with a minimum of worry.

For holiday giving and entertaining a bulging freezer is also a necessity. From Thanksgiving until Christmas we spend many mornings baking different batches of holiday goodies. These make wonderful house gifts whenever we are entertained or quick-as-a-wink nibblers when entertaining casual drop-in company. The trick is to get the goodies into the freezer before the children come home from school and polish off most of them!

From May through October another type of seasonal cooking takes place. When such wonderful fruits as strawberries, blueberries, peaches and apples are at their highest point of flavor and lowest point in price you have a combination hard to beat. And what woman can resist such bargains! On a dull February day, when you think you cannot bear another hour of winter, there is nothing as cheering as a blueberry pie from the freezer to remind you that summer will come again—unlikely as it seems.

If all of these suggestions on how to spend your free time(?) have bewildered you we suggest that you begin with the section entitled "The Instant Gourmet." At any time of year such cooked dishes in your freezer give you a lovely feeling of security.

THE ONCE-A-MONTH COOK

Chain Cooking

Are you curious about the definition of "Chain Cooking"? Good, now you'll have to read this chapter to find out that chain cooking does not mean stringing out for a week what would normally take one day—far from it. It is a catch phrase for a method of making

the work of preparing one meal interlock with and benefit later meals. The meals linked in this fashion may be separated in their serving by days, weeks or even months, made possible, of course, by that grand old lady, the freezer.

Another definition of this technique is "cooking too much on purpose." This method cuts down on shopping time, fuel, work and money. The plan is to relate or overlap your cooking from one dish to another. For example, when chickens are on sale at an irresistibly low price, the relatively wise freezer-owner may buy twelve to put away for future consumption, but the really clever owner will also cook them, making a variety of meals. One day she boils a few of the chickens and thereby creates stock. This is that famous stock that all French cookbooks constantly refer to. It is nothing more than super-duper chicken soup! The stock cools in the refrigerator overnight and the next day our clever cook can make cream sauce for chicken in crêpes, chicken Tetrazzini, etc. Some of the scraps of chicken go into the pancake filling and the breast meat is sliced for chicken divan. Any of that beautiful stock remaining should have a few matzo balls added to it to be served as chicken soup to sick neighbors or visiting royalty.

The same sort of cooking is very successful with chopped beef, ham or even French pancakes. When chopped meat is the special at the market, buy at least ten pounds and set aside a day or two to cook it for the freezer. You can make a potful of meat sauce, freezing some of it as is and using the rest in such dishes as lasagna and veal Parmesan.

Since freezers came along, the definition of eternity is no longer "a ham and two people"! Ham lends itself beautifully to chain cooking and freezing. Buy a whole ham; have the butcher cut it in half. Then after cooking all of it, you can freeze one half as is and grind, slice, cube and julienne the remaining half.

If you raised your eyebrows when we mentioned French pancakes, otherwise known as crêpes, please lower them. They are a cinch to make, including the ones known as Suzette, and they freeze beautifully. For hors d'oeuvres or luncheons fill them with creamed chicken or crabmeat. Will your friends think you're elegant!

You might want to share these secrets with a friend and thereby gain a cooking companion. With two girls in the kitchen it is much easier to cook in quantity and a not-to-be-missed opportunity to gossip—without interruptions. If nothing else spurs you on to quantity cooking this certainly should.

Chicken Chain Cooking

CHICKEN STOCK. To make stock (chicken soup)

Use about one cup of water per pound of chicken (the richer the broth, the better), 2 or 3 carrots, 3 ribs celery, 1 sliced onion, salt and pepper to taste. Cook 45 to 60 minutes, depending on the age of the bird. Strain the stock; if you wish it to be fat-free, refrigerate the stock until it congeals; remove the fat layer from the top. (It freezes beautifully as is.)

You now have stock and a cooked chicken or chickens. You can utilize them in a variety of dishes to freeze or you can freeze them as is for use later.

CHICKEN TETRAZZINI
(8 servings)

Perfect for a large crowd at any time or buffet.

In a large kettle combine

  2 cups stock with enough water to make 6 quarts

Add

  3 tablespoons salt

Cover and bring to a boil, add

  1¼ pounds spaghettini

Cook 6 minute. Drain, place in large baking dish. In skillet melt

  4 tablespoons butter

Add and sauté until soft

  ¾ pound sliced mushrooms

Sprinkle with

  1½ tablespoons lemon juice   ¾ teaspoon salt

Pour mushrooms over spaghettini. In the skillet, brown

  ½ cup sliced almonds   2 tablespoons butter

Drain and add almonds to spaghettini. Melt, then remove from heat

  4 tablespoons butter

Stir in

  2 tablespoons flour   ½ teaspoon pepper
  ¼ teaspoon paprika   ⅛ teaspoon nutmeg
  1½ teaspoons salt

Return to low heat, add slowly, stirring constantly

  ¼ cup sherry   2 cups chicken stock

Cook and stir until thickened

  1 cup heavy cream

Remove from heat, and combine with

Meat from 5-pound cooked chicken

Place on top of spaghettini. Chill quickly and freeze. When ready to serve, defrost, sprinkle with

1 cup freshly grated Parmesan   Paprika to taste
cheese

Bake at 350° about 45 to 60 minutes.

CHICKEN DIVAN
(12 servings)

Place in two 3-quart casseroles or one 6-quart casserole

4 packages frozen broccoli spears, cooked according to directions page 50

Place on top of broccoli

4 cups of cooked chicken, sliced (white meat preferred)

Melt over low heat

¾ cup butter   ¾ cup flour

Gradually stir in and cook slowly, stirring, until thickened

6 cups milk

Add to sauce

1 cup heavy cream   2 jiggers sherry
2 cups shredded Parmesan cheese   1 teaspoon Worcestershire sauce
2⅔ tablespoons prepared m   Salt and pepper to taste
4 tablespoons minced onion

Stir over low heat until cheese is melted. Pour sauce over chicken and broccoli. Chill quickly and freeze. When ready to serve, defrost and bake at 400° for 45 minutes. Before bringing to the table dash generously with

Sherry

CHICKEN IN CRÊPES
(12 crêpes)

Filling:

Melt

5 tablespoons butter

Stir in, off fire

5 tablespoons flour

Cook until lightly browned. Stir in gradually

1 cup hot milk   1 cup hot chicken stock

Cook, stirring until thickened. Cover over low flame 25 minutes, stirring occasionally. Sauté until lightly browned

4 tablespoons chopped mushrooms

in

1 tablespoon butter

Add

3 chopped shallots

Cook another minute. Combine with

2 cups chicken, diced and cooked   ¾ of the cream sauce
3 tablespoons sherry

Spread mixture on

12 crêpes (See page 90) and roll up jelly-roll fashion. Freeze.

To remaining sauce add

1 egg yolk, beaten   4 tablespoons heavy cream

Chill quickly and freeze. When ready to serve, defrost and place crêpes, at room temperature, in shallow greased baking dish. Heat sauce and pour over crêpes. Top with grated Parmesan cheese. Bake at 400° 10 to 15 minutes.

MATZO BALLS FOR CHICKEN SOUP
FEATHERY LIGHT

Combine

¼ cup matzo meal (available at most supermarkets)	1 tablespoon chicken fat
1 beaten egg	1 tablespoon water
	½ teaspoon salt

Set in refrigerator for 20 minutes. Shape into balls about 1½ inches in diameter. Boil in salted water for 20 minutes, covered. Matzo balls may be frozen in the soup. When ready to serve, defrost sufficiently to remove from container and heat through.

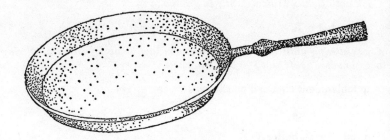

Crêpes Chain Cooking

CRÊPES (FRENCH PANCAKES)
(12 crêpes)

In a small bowl stir with wire whisk until quite smooth

4 heaping tablespoons flour	3 tablespoons milk
1 egg	1 tablespoon vegetable oil
1 egg yolk	

Use enough from

1 cup milk (to make batter of thin consistency)

Refrigerate for 3 to 4 hours. (It may be kept in refrigerator up to a week.) Remove and add enough of remaining milk to reduce again to thin consistency, between light and heavy cream. Heat 6- or 7-inch frying pan (crêpe); when very hot wipe out with piece of slightly buttered waxed paper. Return to lowered heat. Cover bottom of pan with very thin layer of batter. (Pour off any excess.) Cook until golden on one side; turn and cook until golden on other side. Stack them as they cook. Using the same piece of waxed paper rebuttering it occasionally, rub the bottom of the pan between each crêpe.

Freeze crêpes, stacked, and fill them after defrosting, or use them for any recipes calling for crêpes and freeze them filled.

CRÊPES FILLED WITH CRABMEAT
(12 crêpes)

Filling:

Melt

2 tablespoons butter

Remove from heat and stir in

2 tablespoons flour

Return to low heat and stir in carefully

½ cup milk
½ cup vegetable stock (can be made with 1 vegetable-bouillon cube)

Return to low heat and cook, stirring until smooth and thickened. Season with

Salt   Paprika

Melt

3 tablespoons butter

Add and sauté

6 finely chopped shallots

Add and stir gently

½ pound crabmeat

Take from heat and add to sauce with

2 beaten egg yolks   1 tablespoon chives, finely
1 tablespoon Madeira   chopped

Cool combined mixtures. Spread mixture on crêpes and roll up, jelly-roll fashion. If they are to be used as hors d'oeuvres, cut them into thirds. Freeze. When ready to serve, defrost and heat in top of double boiler. Serve from chafing dish.

CRÊPES FOURRÉES
(6 servings)

Make crêpes according to recipe, page 90.

Filling:

Peel, core and cook in water to cover until tender

4 or 5 large cooking apples, cut in large slices

Drain and place in pan with

2 to 3 tablespoons peach or apricot jam	Grated rind of 1 lemon 1 tablespoon sugar

Cook slowly until soft. Place this filling between each of 12 crêpes, piling one crêpe on top of the other like a cake. Cut into six pie-shaped wedges.

Topping:

Combine and mix

Grated rind of 1 orange	3 tablespoons apricot or peach
Grated rind of 1 lemon	jam
Juice of both the orange and the	3 tablespoons sugar
lemon	½ cup water

Freeze the filled crêpes and the topping separately. To serve, defrost both; reheat the crêpes in a 350° oven. Cook the topping in a pan until syrupy in consistency. Pour over heated crêpes and sprinkle with

⅓ cup blanched slivered toasted almonds

Dust with

Confectioners' sugar

CRÊPES SUZETTE
(6 servings)

This is the genuine article guaranteed to make you a famous hostess! Make crêpes according to recipe, page 90.

Sauce Mixture:

Rub until flavor oils are absorbed

  6 cubes of lump sugar

over

  1 lemon peel   1 orange peel

Dissolve sugar in

  ½ cup orange juice, strained

Cream

  ½ cup butter   2 tablespoons confectioners' sugar

Place in saucepan and bring to boil. Add

  1 jigger brandy   2 tablespoons rum
  1 jigger curaçao

Flame it and add the rest of the ingredients. Refrigerate until serving time.

Butter Mixture:

Cream

  6 tablespoons softened butter   3 tablespoons curaçao

Continue creaming while adding

  6 tablespoons confectioners' sugar

You may freeze this mixture or spread the crêpes with it, roll, and freeze. To serve, defrost, heat the sauce on the stove and transfer to chafing dish, or heat in chafing dish. Heat crêpes thoroughly in boiling sauce. Add

  1 jigger brandy   2 tablespoons rum
  4 tablespoons curaçao

When hot, flame with match. Serve while still flaming.

There are a great many steps to this dish, but as you can see, the tasks can be divided and prepared on different days. Making crêpes is a wonderful occupation for two chatty cooks. Utilize two or four saucepans, making lots of batter and crêpes by the dozens. Crêpes are so easy and produce so many elegant dishes.

Ground Beef Chain Cooking

MEAT SAUCE
(about 16 cups)

Heat in sauce pan

  ¼ cup olive oil

Add and brown lightly

  8 crushed garlic cloves   4 pounds ground beef
  2 cups chopped onion   (chuck, round, etc.)

Add

  4 #2½ cans tomatoes   4 bay leaves
  4 tablespoons salt   8 6-ounce cans tomato paste

Simmer, covered, 2½ to 3 hours, until thickened and reduced.

SPAGHETTI AND MEAT SAUCE

  Cook spaghetti according to package directions. Serve with some of above meat sauce and sprinkle with grated Parmesan cheese.

LASAGNA
(6 to 8 servings)

Add to

  4 cups meat sauce (see above)   1½ teaspoons oregano
  1 minced garlic clove

Cook according to package directions

  1 box lasagna noodles

Drain and separate noodles on paper towel.

You will also need

  2 pounds ricotta cheese   8 ounces mozzarella cheese,
  1 cup Parmesan cheese, grated   thinly sliced

Cover bottom of casserole with several spoonfuls of meat sauce. Top with crisscross layer of noodles, then ricotta, mozzarella, sauce and Parmesan. Repeat layering, ending with sauce and topping with mozzarella. Freeze. To serve, defrost and bake at 350° for 50 minutes.

VEAL PARMESAN
(6 to 8 servings)

Dip

2 pounds veal cutlets (Italian-style—cut very thin and pounded)

into mixture of

Seasoned bread crumbs   Grated Parmesan cheese

then into mixture of

3 beaten eggs   Salt and pepper to taste

then into crumbs again. Brown slices on each side in

⅓ cup olive oil

Alternate in casserole layers of

Cutlets   2 packages mozzarella cheese,
4 cups meat sauce   sliced

Top with sauce. Freeze. To serve, defrost and bake at 350° for 30 to 45 minutes. Cheese should be browned.

Also see the section on cooking a week at a time for other uses of Ground Beef:

Chafing Dish Meatballs and Franks (p. 140)
Hamburg Surprise (p. 33)
Meat Loaf Ring (p. 43)
Moussaka (p. 37)
Picadillo (p. 39)
Swiss Meat Roll (p. 34)

We have suggested just a few ways to chain cook. Many recipes in other sections of the book are adaptable to this type of cooking. You will know what kind of chain cooking fits in best with your family's tastes and the things you prefer to serve to your guests. In this kind of cooking one good thing leads to another. In fact, you will have to set limits or you will find that making lasagna might somehow lead to making mincemeat pie!

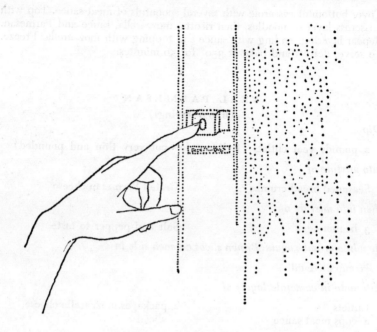

THE INSTANT GOURMET

Unexpected Guests

What a warm and friendly feeling you can have toward those surprise visitors when your trusty old freezer is well prepared for the emergency. There are certain dishes we always try to keep on hand, prepared and frozen.

A whole meal, and a darn good one at that, can pop right out of the freezer and be ready in a jiffy. Don't forget the cocktail nibbles to keep your guests occupied while the rest of the food is cooking. We have suggested hors d'oeuvres that can be ready in less than half an hour. In the main course department a Crab and Mushroom Casserole, Shrimp 'n' Oysters or Chicken Livers Risotto (recipes included) should be waiting at all times in any well-stocked freezer, for these particular dishes can cook successfully without defrosting and be ready in less than one hour. The commercially frozen rock lobster tails are marvelous to keep in the freezer—buy them on sale—and can be quickly made into a really elegant meal with a lemon butter sauce (p. 69). Even plain old hamburgers can quickly be made into something special with the Hamburgers Diane recipe (p. 104).

A loaf of French onion bread is a wonderful item to keep on hand for emergencies and should be kept wrapped in aluminum foil in which it can be baked. As a matter of fact, all rolls or breads defrost quickly and are great for filling up the guests! With a salad of ingredients on hand or a quickly cooked frozen vegetable, your meal is almost complete.

There are so many quick-defrosting desserts, a few of which are listed here; others are scattered throughout the book. Some of them are equally appropriate if people drop in unexpectedly just for the evening.

Pound cake is one of the best cakes to keep for this type of situation. It will defrost quickly if sliced and needs no frosting or last-minute trimming, though it is a natural with ice cream. The latter, it goes without saying, is always in your freezer for any occasion. Don't forget the commercially frozen puff pastries or your own cream puffs frozen filled with whipped cream. With such an array of foods in your freezer this "knight in gleaming porcelain" will rescue you every time—all you have to do is put the food in and take it out!

WIFE-SAVER MENU NO. 1

* CREAM PUFFS FILLED
* CRAB AND MUSHROOM CASSEROLE
FROZEN VEGETABLE
HONEYBUNS (p. 214)
* POUND CAKE
BEVERAGE

CREAM PUFFS
(12 large, 50 to 60 miniature)

Heat oven to 400°

Bring to boil in a heavy pan

  1 cup water

Reduce to low heat. Add all at once

  ¼ pound butter   1 cup sifted flour
  ½ teaspoon salt

Cook, stirring vigorously until mixture leaves sides of pan and forms compact ball. Remove from heat. Cool slightly. Add, one at a time, beating after each addition until smooth and glossy

  4 eggs

Drop on ungreased cookie sheets by teaspoon or tablespoon, depending on size desired. Bake 30 minutes for miniatures, 45 minutes for larger ones. When cooled, cut off tops and fill. The puffs may also be frozen unfilled, refreshed in the oven and then filled.

Hors d'oeuvre Fillings:

Cream Cheese and Ham

Combine

  6 ounces cream cheese
  1 3-ounce can deviled ham
  Catsup to moisten

Cream Cheese and Roquefort

Combine

  3 ounces cream cheese
  Roquefort to taste
  Sherry to moisten

Fill puffs and freeze. To serve it is not necessary to defrost. Place them in a 400° oven for 15 to 20 minutes.

CRAB AND MUSHROOM CASSEROLE
(6 servings)

Sauté for 5 minutes and set aside

  1 pound sliced mushrooms   2 tablespoons butter

Melt

  6 tablespoons butter

Remove from heat and blend in

⅓ cup flour

Add

10-ounce can chicken broth   Salt and pepper to taste
1½ cups medium or light cream

Return to heat and cook until thickened and smooth.

In 6-cup casserole arrange in alternate layers

Mushrooms   1½ pounds fresh or 2 cans
Sauce   crabmeat

Sprinkle with

Buttered bread crumbs   Grated American cheese

Freeze. To serve, put frozen casserole in 325° oven. Bake until brown
and bubbly, 45 to 60 minutes. Defrosted casserole bakes at 350° for 30
minutes.

POUND CAKE
(makes 2 cakes)

Cream until very light

2 cups butter (*no substitutes*)

Add little by little, beating constantly

2 cups sugar

Beat in

1 teaspoon vanilla   2 tablespoons brandy

Add, 1 at a time, beating constantly

9 eggs

Sift

4 cups sifted flour

with

½ teaspoon mace   ½ teaspoon salt
½ teaspoon cream of tartar

Add slowly to batter, beating. Use two bread loaf tins, buttered and lined with waxed paper. Bake at 325° for 60 minutes. Cool and freeze. If you want to use the cake quickly, freeze it sliced, but place paper between each slice and wrap doubly well to prevent drying out. The slices will defrost in 10 minutes or can be popped in the toaster. Delicious served with butter, jam or ice cream.

WIFE-SAVER MENU NO. 2

* PASTRY SNAILS
* SHRIMP 'N' OYSTERS
HEAT-AND-SERVE ROLLS
SALAD
* MERINGUE SHELLS
ICE CREAM AND FRUITS
BEVERAGE

PASTRY SNAILS
(50 slices)

Sift together

¾ cup flour
Dash salt

Cut in

¼ cup shortening

Add

2 tablespoons cold water

Work into stiff dough. Refrigerate for ½ hour. Then roll to very thin rectangle on top of waxed paper. Spread with mixture of

6-ounce can deviled ham   Pickle relish if desired
1 tablespoon mustard

Roll as for jelly roll. Freeze. When ready to serve, slice thin. Bake at 400° for 15 minutes. Serve hot.

SHRIMP 'N' OYSTERS
(8 servings)

Place in buttered casserole

2 10- to 12-ounce packages frozen peeled shrimp, slightly thawed
2 cans frozen oysters, thawed
2 cups wild rice
2 #2 cans tomatoes

2 medium onions, chopped
2 tablespoons basil
2 bay leaves
Salt and pepper to taste
1 cup water

Cover tightly and bake at 325° for 1 hour. Cool quickly and freeze. To serve, place frozen casserole in 325° oven and bake for 45 to 60 minutes.

MERINGUE SHELLS, ICE CREAM AND FRUITS

Sift

1½ cups sugar

Beat until half stiff

7 egg whites   ⅛ teaspoon salt

Add the sugar, 1 tablespoon at a time, beating constantly. Continue to beat several minutes after the last of the sugar has been added. Add

1 teaspoon vanilla

Fold in ¾ cup sugar

Place large spoonfuls of this mixture on a baking sheet covered with waxed paper or shape with pastry bag into ovals. Make slight depression in center with back of spoon. Bake at 225° for 45 to 60 minutes. Remove from sheet and while still warm, crush in the center with thumb to make depression for filling. Freeze.

To serve, defrost (will defrost in less than 1 hour at room temperature) and fill with

Ice cream   Frozen fruit, just thawed

WIFE-SAVER MENU NO. 3

CHEESE SAVORIES (p. 142)
* CHICKEN LIVERS RISOTTO
SALAD
* CRUNCH STICKS
* CHOCOLATE COCONUT CRUST WITH ICE CREAM

CHICKEN LIVERS RISOTTO
(6 servings)

In

¼ cup olive oil

Cook until brown, stirring constantly

1 cup rice

Add

1 small onion, chopped	Salt to taste
2 cups chicken stock	Pinch of saffron
1 clove garlic, crushed	¼ teaspoon powdered ginger

Cover pan tightly and simmer 20 minutes over low heat, until liquid is absorbed. Meanwhile quickly sauté

1½ pounds chicken livers	¼ cup butter
½ pound mushrooms, sliced thin	

Add livers, mushrooms and pan juices to rice. Mix thoroughly. Freeze quickly. To serve, defrost at room temperature if you have time or by cooking in top of double boiler; adjust seasonings. Sprinkle with

¼ cup grated Parmesan cheese	Coarsely ground black pepper

CRUNCH STICKS
(Makes 20)

Cut in half

Biscuits

from 1 refrigerator package. Roll each half into pencil-thin stick, about 4 inches long

Brush with

Milk

Mix together in shallow pan

1½ cups crisp rice cereal, coarsely crushed	2 tablespoons dill weed
2 tablespoons sesame seeds	1 tablespoon celery seed
	2 teaspoons salt

Roll sticks in mixture. Bake on greased baking sheet at 450° for 5 minutes. Freeze. To serve, defrost and bake at 450° for 5 minutes, until golden.

CHOCOLATE COCONUT CRUST
WITH ICE CREAM
(6 servings)

In top of double boiler melt

2 squares unsweetened chocolate	2 tablespoons butter

Combine

2 tablespoons hot milk	⅔ cup sifted confectioners' sugar

Add to chocolate mixture and stir well. Add

1½ cups coconut, toasted

Spread on bottom and sides of greased 9-inch pie pan. Freeze. To serve, defrost (will defrost in less than 1 hour at room temperature) and fill with your choice of

Vanilla, peppermint stick, pistachio ice cream, etc.

WIFE-SAVER MENU NO. 4

* SHELBY'S CHEESE STICKS
* HAMBURGERS DIANE
FRENCH FRIES, FROZEN
FROZEN VEGETABLE
* CREAM PUFFS OR PUFF PASTRY FILLED WITH
WHIPPED CREAM OR ICE CREAM
BEVERAGE

SHELBY'S CHEESE STICKS
(48 sticks)

An excellent cook's excellent recipe

Mix

1 cup sifted flour
½ teaspoon salt
½ teaspoon sugar
½ teaspoon ginger
½ teaspoon monosodium glutamate

¼ cup sesame seeds, toasted lightly
1 cup extra sharp cheese, grated

Mix

1 egg yolk, beaten
2 tablespoons water

½ teaspoon Worcestershire sauce
⅓ cup melted butter

Stir in dry ingredients. Form into soft ball. Chill slightly in refrigerator. Place ball between two sheets of waxed paper. Roll out as for pie crust about ¼ inch thick. Do not use any extra flour for rolling. Cut into strips ¾ of an inch by 3 inches or any desired size. Bake at 350° about 8 minutes or less. Freeze. To serve, defrost.

HAMBURGERS DIANE
(8 servings)

This is an adaptation of the more elegant and famous Steak Diane.

Remove

16 frozen hamburger patties from freezer

Let them defrost as long as possible, but be sure to take this into account when cooking (will defrost completely in about 2 hours at room temperature). Sprinkle over all of them, on both sides

4 tablespoons freshly ground pepper

Press pepper in with heel of your hand. Let stand. When ready to serve, sprinkle bottom of heavy skillet with

Light layer of salt

Turn heat to high and when salt begins to brown slightly, add hamburgers. Cook until well browned on one side, turn and cook over low flame 8 to 12 minutes or until cooked to desired degree.

Place on each patty

2 teaspoons butter

Add

Few drops tabasco   Few dashes lemon juice
Few dashes Worcestershire sauce

Turn heat very low, blaze with

4 tablespoons cognac

Place patties on serving platter and pour sauce over them. Sprinkle with

Parsley   Chives

CREAM PUFFS OR PUFF PASTRY SHELLS
FILLED WITH WHIPPED CREAM OR ICE CREAM

Make large cream puffs according to directions (p. 98).

Cool and fill with

Whipped cream, sweetened

or

Ice cream

Freeze. To serve, defrost for 15 minutes and serve with a hot chocolate sauce (p. 205) or bake puff pastry shells according to package directions. Cool and fill as above.

Other quick-to-fix dishes may be found elsewhere in the book. They include:

Hors d'Oeuvres

Stuffed Mushroom Caps (p. 148)
Smithfield Ham in Biscuits (p. 148)
Clams Normande (p. 142)
Olive Cheese Balls (p. 145)
Quiche Lorraine, Miniature (p. 145)
Sausage Balls in Pastry (p. 147)

Main Dishes

Meat Sauce for Spaghetti (p. 94)
Hamburg Surprise (p. 33)
Cauliflower-Shrimp Dish (p. 68)
Chicken of the Sea (p. 46)
Pizza (p. 225)
Rock Lobster Tails au Beurre (p. 69)
Tempura (p. 69)

Salads

Cheese Fruit Freeze (p. 213)
Strawberry Cottage Cheese Mold (p. 217)
Frozen Waldorf Salad (p. 182)
Grapefruit Avocado Freeze (p. 179)
Red-and-White Mold (p. 171)

Vegetables

Artichokes and Mushrooms (p. 53)
Cauliflower with Black Olives (p. 54)
Corn Pudding (p. 54)
Limas in Cream (p. 56)
Peas Suprême (p. 57)

Starches

Potato Stix Parmesan (p. 57)
Cheesey Baked Potatoes (p. 165)
Garlic Shoestrings (p. 171)
Potato Puffs, Parmesan (p. 57)

Breads

All breads

Desserts

Schnecken (p. 198)
Rolled Cookies (p. 198)
Cinnamon Horns (p. 114)
Apricot Crescents (p. 193)
Toffee Squares (p. 121)
Orange Balls (p. 119)
Florentines (p. 117)
Puff Pastry Turnovers (p. 68)
Fruit Torte (p. 130)
Sour Cream Coffee Cake (p. 120)
Pecan Tartes (p. 197)
Any desserts from the frozen section

Sugar 'n' Spice

Holiday Baking

Sugar and spice make up little girls—add butter and cream, chocolate and vanilla and you make up the wonderful aromas coming from the kitchen a month or so before the end-of-year holidays. Before the freezer came to our house we were limited to baking only what could be stored in tightly closed tins for a month. Now that so many marvelous cakes can be stored in tightly closed freezers for months in advance of the busy holiday season, you can begin working in August if you wish!

With the last morsel of Thanksgiving turkey packed away until your family can face it again, Christmas cooking begins in earnest. You may even have started your fruitcakes before.

A dandy place to begin your master plan would be in the grocery store with a master list of ingredients. Then clear the kitchen decks for action and bake away! We try to bake a batch a day as soon as the breakfast dishes are done. It hardly seems to interrupt the busier-than-normal schedule that accompanies the holiday season.

All but a few samples can be tucked away in the freezer before the samplers come home from school or office. (By far the worst snitchers in our families are our husbands!)

Be sure to share these wonderful goodies with the people on your gift list. The work of your own hands adds doubly to holiday pleasures. There are endless varieties of wrappings to be found in the five-and-ten that make pretty and useful packages: baking tins, clay flowerpots, apothecary jars, straw baskets that you can decorate yourself with paint, colored aluminum foil, felt cutouts, sparkles or anything that tickles your fancy.

Label your gifts, especially if they must be kept frozen or refrigerated.

And make enough for your own family to forestall anguished cries as the packages leave the house. Keep them, too, for drop-in company and drop-in visiting.

We think the cinnamon horns, croissant and yeast dough recipes deserve special mention—they have become traditions in our homes for Christmas morning breakfast. After you have tasted them you are welcome to adopt these traditions as your own.

APPLESAUCE BREAD MARLOWE

Beat

  1 egg

Add and beat

  1 cup well-seasoned applesauce   2 tablespoons melted shortening
                                         (*not* butter)

Add, sifted together

  2 cups sifted flour   1 teaspoon salt
  ¾ cup sugar   ½ teaspoon baking soda
  1 tablespoon baking powder   ½ teaspoon cinnamon

Add

  1 cup coarsely chopped walnuts

Stir all just until blended. Pour into greased 9 x 3 x 5-inch loaf pan. Bake
for 1 hour at 350° or until crust cracks. Freeze. Defrost to serve.

APRICOT FRUITCAKE

In a small saucepan bring to a boil

  1 cup dried apricots, cut into   Water to cover
    small pieces

Cook one minute. Drain off liquid. Cool. Meanwhile cream

  ¾ cup butter   1 cup sugar

Blend in

  4 egg yolks

Sift and measure

  2 cups flour

Use half of flour to coat

  1 pound mixed candied fruit   ⅓ cup sliced candied cherries
  1 cup golden raisins   ⅓ cup diced candied pineapple
  ⅓ cup chopped almonds

Add to creamed mixture with

  1 teaspoon salt   1 teaspoon grated lemon or
                                        orange peel

Dissolve

    ½ teaspoon baking soda

in

    2 tablespoons hot water

Beat until stiff

    4 egg whites

Add soda to batter. Add egg whites alternately with remainder of flour. Butter 10-inch tube pan, line bottom with brown paper and butter again. Pour batter in and bake at 275° for 2 hours and 15 minutes. Have shallow pan of water in bottom of oven. Let cake cool on wire rack in tube pan. Remove from pan and seal airtight in two layers of heavy-duty foil for at least two weeks. Freeze after that. Defrost to serve.

BRIOCHES

Don't run away because you see yeast. The directions are quite explicit and the result is worth the effort.

Dissolve

    1 package dry yeast or 1 cake yeast

in

    ¼ cup lukewarm water

Stir to dissolve. Add yeast mixture to

    ½ cup flour

in small bowl. Stir with spoon until it forms a stiff ball. Turn out on lightly floured board. Knead a little until you get a smooth surface on top. Cup dough in your hands to make round top and cut halfway through ball with sharp knife in the shape of an "X" like a hot cross bun. Open each of four petals a little. Drop it into a 4-cup pitcher half filled with lukewarm water and leave it to rise to the top of the water. This will happen in 3 to 7 minutes. In the meantime in large mixing bowl beat until light and fluffy

    5 ounces sweet butter

Remove butter with rubber scraper, cleaning bowl thoroughly with scraper. Place butter aside. In mixer, place

1½ cups unsifted flour	1 teaspoon salt
1 tablespoon sugar	3 very large or 3½ large eggs

Beat until shiny. Add butter and well-drained yeast dough. Mix all together with spoon and put in floured bowl. Cover dough with Saran wrap and cloth and put into warm place to rise, until double in bulk— ¾ to 1 hour. When risen, stir around top with finger to break the rise. Cover and put in the refrigerator overnight or in the freezer 2 to 3 hours. Remove dough and work quickly so it won't get too sticky to handle. Place on floured board. Shape two-thirds of dough into balls—the size will depend on the size of the muffin tins you use. Regular 3-inch tins take 2-inch balls. Miniature muffin tins take ½-inch to ¾-inch balls. Place the balls in well-buttered muffin tins.

Form an equal number of small balls from remaining third of dough. Shape one end into cone shape. With finger make depression in center of large ball and insert tip of cone. Press gently. Cover loosely with towel and let rise in warm place until double in bulk, about 1 hour.

Brioche

Brush lightly with mixture of

1 egg yolk   1 tablespoon milk

Bake at 425° for 15 to 20 minutes for large broiches and 10 to 12 minutes for miniatures. Cool quickly and freeze. To serve, remove from freezer and heat at 300° until thawed and heated through.

BUTTERSCOTCH BARS

Mix

1½ cups sifted flour   ½ cup soft butter
¾ cup brown sugar   ¼ teaspoon salt

Press into 9 x 13-inch pan. Bake at 375° for 10 minutes. Meanwhile combine in double boiler

1 6-ounce package butterscotch bits	2 tablespoons shortening
	1 tablespoon water
¼ cup dark corn syrup	1 teaspoon salt

Stir until smooth. Remove from heat. Blend in

2 cups coarsely chopped walnuts

Spoon over top of cookie layer and spread evenly. Bake at 375° for 8 minutes. Cut into bars while warm. Cool and freeze. Defrost to serve.

BÛCHE DE NOËL

A traditional holiday treat

Beat until light and fluffy

7 egg yolks

Add gradually and beat until very thick and light

1 cup granulated sugar	4 tablespoons cocoa

Fold in

7 stiffly beaten egg whites

Spread batter evenly in jelly-roll pan, buttered and lined with waxed paper. Bake at 350° about 15 minutes. Cover cake with damp towel and let cool for 30 minutes. Loosen from baking sheet and dust generously with

Cocoa

Turn cake out onto two overlapping sheets of waxed paper and remove paper. Spread with

3 tablespoons mocha butter cream	1 cup heavy cream which has been whipped with
	½ cup granulated sugar

Roll up cake lengthwise; lift up one side of waxed paper and flip over about 2 inches onto itself. Continue to roll by lifting paper. Slide it onto long wooden board or oblong cake plate. Spread rest of mocha butter cream over roll with spatula and with tine of fork imitate bark of tree. Freeze. To serve, defrost.

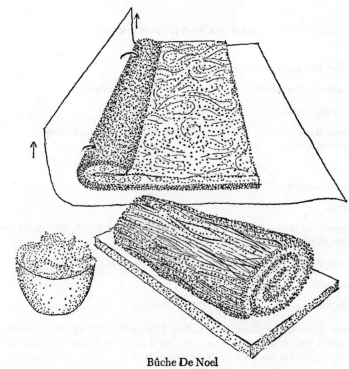

Bûche De Noel

Mocha Butter Cream:

In top of double boiler mix

5 tablespoons sugar   1 cup hot milk
2 egg yolks

Stir with wooden spoon until it is coated. Do not boil. Strain custard into bowl and cool. In the meantime dissolve

2 tablespoons instant coffee

in

2 tablespoons water

Soften

1 cup sweet butter

Gradually work in custard and coffee to make smooth light cream. Use wire whisk.

CINNAMON HORNS
(2 dozen)

Combine, stir until dissolved and set aside

1 package dry yeast   ¼ cup warm water

Mix as for pie crust

2 cups flour, sifted   1 tablespoon shortening
¼ pound butter   Dash salt

Add

2 beaten eggs   Yeast mixture

Mix well.

Refrigerate at least 2 hours. Divide dough into 3 parts. Roll each part out into circle on waxed paper covered with

¼ cup sugar   2 teaspoons cinnamon

Spread with

Nuts   Raisins

Cut into 8 pie wedges and roll starting from wide end up to point. Place on greased cookie sheets and let rise for 1 hour in warm place. Bake at 400° for 15 to 20 minutes. Cool and freeze.

CROISSANTS

These are worth every bit of time they take. No other roll tastes as good.

Combine and let stand 5 to 10 minutes, until dissolved

1 cake compressed yeast   ¼ cup lukewarm water

Meanwhile scald

1 cup milk

Pour scalded milk into large bowl and stir in

1 tablespoon sugar   1 teaspoon salt

Cool to lukewarm. Stir softened yeast and add with about

3 cups sifted flour

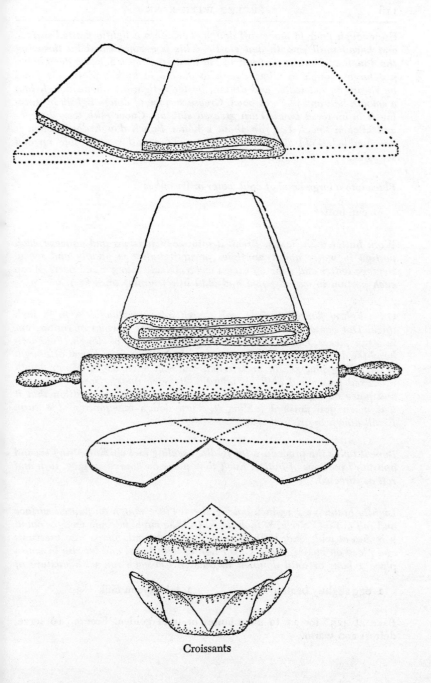

Croissants

Use enough flour to make soft dough. Turn onto a lightly floured surface and knead until smooth and elastic. This is accomplished by throwing the dough against the pastry board at least 100 times. Select a deep bowl, just large enough to allow dough to double in bulk. (Warm the bowl by rinsing in hot water and drying; butter it lightly.) Shape dough into a smooth ball and place in bowl. Grease surface of dough lightly by turning it in buttered bowl. Turn greased side up. Cover with waxed paper and kitchen towel. Let rise about 2 hours. Punch dough down when it has doubled. Fold sides toward center. Turn ball smooth side up and set aside.

Place into a large bowl of cold water or ice cubes

¾ cup butter

Work butter with hands. Break it into small portions and squeeze each portion in water about 20 times or until butter is pliable and waxy. Remove butter and wipe off excess water. Divide into 3 equal parts. Wrap each portion in waxed paper and chill in refrigrator until firm.

On a lightly floured surface, roll dough into a rectangle ¼ to ½ inch thick. Dot center third of rolled dough with one portion of butter, cut in small pieces. Cover butter with right-hand third of dough. Fold left-hand third of dough over that. You now have three even layers of dough. With rolling pin, gently press down and seal open edges. Wrap dough in waxed paper and chill 30 minutes. Remove dough from refrigerator and place on lightly floured surface in exactly the same position that it was when you finished folding it. Turn dough one-quarter of a turn. Reroll dough to original size.

Repeat twice the procedure for folding, sealing and chilling, using second and third portions of butter. Each time place on floured surface, turn and roll as directed.

Lightly butter 12 x 15-inch baking sheet. Place dough on floured surface and roll out into circle, ¼ inch thick. Cut the circle into pie wedges about 3 inches at wide end. Roll up starting at wide end. Shape into crescents and place on baking sheet. Cover lightly with towel and let rise in warm place 1 hour or until doubled in bulk. Brush each roll with mixture of

1 egg slightly beaten   1 tablespoon milk

Bake at 425° for 15 to 20 minutes or until golden. Freeze. To serve, defrost and warm.

FLORENTINES
(4 dozen)

These sell at one fancy bakery for 25¢ each.

Stir together until well blended

¾ cup heavy cream   ¼ cup sugar

Stir in

¼ cup flour, sifted   ½ pound candied orange peel,
½ cup slivered almonds   very finely chopped
   (blanched and toasted)

Drop dough by heaping teaspoonfuls on heavily greased and floured baking sheet. Flatten cookie with knife. Bake at 350° for 10 to 12 minutes, or just until cookies are lightly brown around edges. Leave cookies on baking sheet a few minutes to firm. Remove with spatula and cool. Over hot water melt

2 4-ounce excellent sweet chocolate bars

Turn cookies upside down; cover bottom with chocolate.
Allow to dry several hours at room temperature, until chocolate becomes firm. Freeze. Defrost to serve.

FRUIT KUCHEN

Blend together as for a pie crust

2½ cups flour   ⅓ cup sugar
2½ teaspoons baking powder   1 teaspoon salt
1 cup butter

Add and blend in

2 eggs (reserve 2 teaspoons white)   ¼ cup milk

Roll half of dough on floured board and fit into buttered 9 x 15-inch Pyrex dish.

Grate coarsely

9 apples (you may substitute peaches or berries)

Add

¾ cup sugar   1 teaspoon cinnamon
Juice and grated rind of 1 lemon

Place fruit mixture on top of dough. Cover with remaining dough.

Brush top with

  Egg white

Sprinkle with

  Cinnamon   ½ cup chopped nuts
  Sugar

Pat down. Bake at 350° for 45 minutes. Cool and freeze. When ready to serve, defrost and reheat a few minutes. Serve warm.

HOLIDAY ICE CREAM CAKE
(12 servings)

In large bowl combine

  1 pound crumbled almond   ½ cup whole maraschino
    macaroons   cherries
  1 cup pecans, chopped   ½ cup sherry

Make layers in 9-inch spring form of

  Macaroon mixture   1 quart chocolate ice cream
  1 quart butter pecan ice cream   Macaroon mixture
  Macaroon mixture

Freeze. To serve, allow to soften sufficiently so that it is easy to cut.

OATMEAL TOLL HOUSE COOKIES

Beat until blended

  ½ cup butter   ½ teaspoon vanilla
  6 tablespoons granulated sugar   ¼ teaspoon water
  6 tablespoons brown sugar

Beat in

  1 egg

Add

  ¾ cup sifted flour   ½ teaspoon salt
  ½ teaspoon baking soda

Stir in

1 cup uncooked rolled oats   1 cup semisweet chocolate bits

Drop by teaspoonfuls onto greased cookie sheets. Bake at 375° for 8 minutes. Cool and freeze. Defrost to serve.

ORANGE BALLS
(3 dozen)

Combine

1 7½-ounce package vanilla   ¾ cup grated coconut
  wafers, crushed   ¾ cup confectioners' sugar

Add and mix well

½ cup frozen orange juice concentrate, thawed

Form into 1-inch balls. Roll half of ball in

Additional confectioners' sugar

Freeze. Defrost to serve.

PLUM PUDDING

Begin weeks or months before Christmas. Nothing short of fabulous.

In a large bowl mix thoroughly

1 cup finely chopped suet
1½ cups fine dry bread crumbs
¾ cup flour
½ cup seeded raisins ⎫
½ cup currants   ⎬ washed and then steeped in a little brandy
½ cup sultanas   ⎭ for 1 hour

¼ cup finely diced preserved   ¼ cup blanched almonds
  orange rind   ⅔ cup sugar
¼ cup finely diced preserved   ¾ teaspoon cinnamon
  lemon rind   ½ teaspoon nutmeg
¼ cup finely diced preserved   ½ teaspoon salt
  citron   ¼ teaspoon ground cloves
⅜ cup finely chopped apple   ¼ teaspoon mace
2½ tablespoons chopped preserved   Juice and grated rind of 1 orange
  ginger   Juice and grated rind of ½ lemon
¼ cup finely chopped dried figs

Sprinkle the ingredients with

　1 cup brandy

Blend well. Cover bowl with towel and put in refrigerator for 6 to 8 days at least, adding a few spoonfuls of brandy and tossing mixture each day.

Then stir in

　6 beaten eggs

Pack firmly into buttered mold or coffee cans, two-thirds full, cover closely and steam. Place mold or cans on rack or trivet over 1 inch boiling water in steamer or heavy kettle. Cover kettle closely. Use high heat at first and as steam begins to escape reduce to low. If all in one mold, steam for 5 hours. Cool and freeze. To serve, defrost and heat by same method used to steam, steaming for 1 hour.

To serve, sprinkle with

　Fine granulated sugar

Pour over

　4 ounces warmed brandy

Flame and serve with Hard Sauce.

Hard Sauce:

Cream in small bowl at high speed

　⅓ cup butter

Gradually add

　1 cup confectioners' sugar

Blend well and add

　⅛ teaspoon salt   1 teaspoon brandy

Beat until sauce is creamy, about 5 minutes. Freeze. To serve, defrost. May be cut into individual serving pieces.

SOUR CREAM COFFEE CAKE
(8 servings)

Cream together

　1¼ cups sugar   ½ pound butter

3 eggs
2½ cups self-rising flour
1 teaspoon baking powder ⎫
1 teaspoon baking soda   ⎬ sifted together
1 teaspoon vanilla   ⎭   ½ pint sour cream

Combine

1 cup finely chopped nuts   2 teaspoons cinnamon
¼ cup sugar

Put half of batter in 9-inch spring form. Sprinkle with half of nut mixture. Add rest of batter, then rest of nut mixture. Bake at 350° for 1 hour. Cool quickly and freeze. To serve, defrost and warm, or defrost by warming in 300° oven.

TOFFEE SQUARES
(40 squares)

Cream until fluffy

1 cup butter   1 cup packed brown sugar

Beat in

1 egg yolk   1 teaspoon vanilla

Stir in

2 cups flour, sifted

Spread thinly in 9 x 13-inch pan. Bake at 350° for 15 to 20 minutes. Melt in top of double boiler

6 ounces semisweet chocolate

Spread on warm cookie surface. Sprinkle with

1 cup chopped nuts

Cut into squares when cool and freeze. Defrost to serve.

YEAST DOUGH

Dissolve

  2 packages compressed yeast

in

  ½ cup warm milk

Beat together until lemon-colored

  3 eggs   ½ cup sugar

Add yeast mixture and

  4 cups sifted flour

alternately with

  ½ pound melted butter

Cover and refrigerate overnight.
Roll out half the dough into a ¼-inch thick circle on a floured board.

Spread with

  Melted butter

Spread with cheese mixture on one edge. Then roll up like jelly roll. Place on greased baking sheet. Cover and let rise in warm place until double in bulk, about 2 hours. Spread generously with melted butter. Bake at 350° for 30 minutes until well browned. Cool and freeze. Defrost and reheat to serve.

Cheese Filling:

Press through ricer or strainer

  ½ pound farmer cheese

Mix with

  1 egg   1 teaspoon soft butter
  1 tablespoon sugar   Pinch salt

Pecan Filling:

Roll remaining dough into same size circle. Suread with
  Melt butter

Sprinkle with

    Cinnamon   **Sugar**

Place in each cup of muffin tins

    ½ teaspoon melted butter   1 teaspoon brown sugar

Place in bottom of tin

    1 whole pecan

Roll circle up like jelly roll. Cut into slices to fit size of cup. Place one slice in each cup. Cover and let rise in warm place until double in bulk. Spread with melted butter. Bake 15 to 20 minutes at 350° depending on size of muffin cups. Cool and freeze. Defrost and reheat to serve.

Additional Holiday Baking Suggestions:

    Chocolate Cheesecake (p. 171)
    Schnecken (p. 198)
    Rolled Cookies (p. 198)
    Pecan Tartes (p. 197)
    Apple Pie (p. 125)
    Blueberry Pie (p. 128)
    Strawberry Rhubarb Pie (p. 132)
    Pound Cake (p. 99)
    Chinese Walnut Cookies (p. 195)
    Apricot Crescents (p. 193)

UP TO DATE IN GRANDMA'S KITCHEN

Freezing Rather Than Canning Seasonal Foods

Grandmother canned all summer so there would be plenty to eat in the winter. She even did some freezing, Eskimo-style, but it was a risky business since the freezer itself might thaw at any time.

Today freezing methods are somewhat more advanced. Freezers keep fairly even temperatures, except when a storm turns off the electricity. Even so, the risks are minimal and freezing is the best

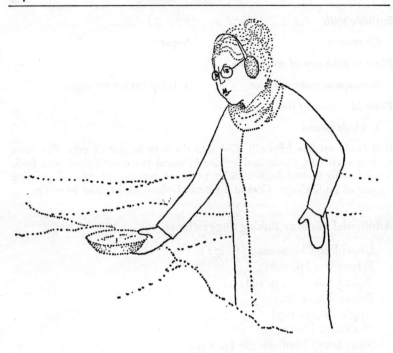

method for preserving most foods in their nearest-to-fresh-tasting state. In many instances, it is the only method. (Whoever heard of canned blueberry pie!)

Summer, however, still remains the best time to take advantage of the wonderfully abundant and fresh produce available in your own local market. A preceding section goes into detail about the proper procedures for freezing fruits and vegetables au naturel, but in this section we'd like to tell you about our favorite recipes that are made in quantity during the seasonal abundance of various fruits. Each of you will probably have local produce peculiar to your area and know many local recipes that you can make in quantity.

As in other quantity cooking, "teaming up" with a friend makes light of such boring tasks as pitting plums or stemming blueberries. And let's face it, how else can you get so many delicious dishes at so reasonable a price? Perhaps you can even do your own berrying in some lovely cool woods, or have an apple or peach tree blooming in your garden. The yield of just one such tree is all a single person can tackle without staying up nights.

With the added incentive of gossiping with a friend, however, it hardly seems like work to make as many as 12 Coffee Cakes in one day. We wish we could say they carry us through the winter, but alas, the last crumb is devoured long before the tulips bloom!

APPLE PIE
(10 servings)

It's just like Mother used to make since it's Mother's recipe.

Prepare pie crust for 11-inch pie plate.
Do not bake. Brush shell with egg white.

Filling:

Pare, core and slice thinly into unbaked pie shell (see p. 126)

8 large cooking applies

Mix together

¾ cup sugar   2 tablespoons lemon juice
Pinch salt

Sprinkle over apples. Dot apples with

1 tablespoon butter

Cover with top crust. Trim the crust so that there is ¼-inch overhang. Wet edge of lower crust and seal crusts together by pinching dough. If you freeze before baking do not cut vents in top crust. Bake frozen pie at 450° for 15 to 20 minutes. After first 10 minutes, remove pie and cut vents in top. Reduce heat to 375° and bake 40 to 45 minutes.

To freeze after baking bake the pie at 450° for 10 minutes. Reduce heat and bake at 350° for 35 minutes more. Freeze after it cools. To serve, defrost and warm in 350° oven about 15 minutes.

PIE CRUSTS
(makes 11-inch bottom crust or 9-inch top and bottom)

Sift together

1½ cups sifted flour   ½ teaspoon salt

Cut in with pastry blender until pieces are the size of small peas

½ cup shortening

Sprinkle with approximately

4 tablespoons cold water one tablespoon at a time

Mix with fork. Repeat until dough is moistened. It is of good consistency when it does not stick to your hands when you gather it up to form into a ball. It will handle more easily if chilled for ½ hour.

Roll out on floured board, turning as you roll. If you wish a baked, unfilled shell, bake empty shell at 450° for 12 to 15 minutes. Before baking prick all over with fork, place piece of waxed paper in shell and weight down with dried beans or rice for first 10 minutes.

Remove and finish baking another 2 to 5 minutes.

You may freeze the crust before or after baking.

APPLESAUCE

Wash, cut into quarters and core

Unpeeled apples with good flavoring

Place in saucepan and partly cover them with water. Stew them until they are tender. Put them through a ricer or food mill. Add enough

Sugar

to suit your taste. Boil puree for 3 minutes.

Chill quickly and freeze in portions suitable to your family's needs. Defrost, and serve warm or cold. If desired sprinkle sauce with cinnamon, nutmeg.

APPLESAUCE WITH CRANBERRIES

Combine and stir

2 cups cranberries, fresh or frozen   ¾ cup water
2 cups quartered apples, cored

Cook until soft over low heat. Put through coarse sieve. Add

1 cup sugar

Cook and stir the puree until sugar dissolves. You may sprinkle with

Grated orange rind

Cool quickly and freeze in portions suitable for your family's needs. To serve, defrost. Serve hot or cold.

CINNAMON APPLE RINGS
(4 dozen slices)

Combine in skillet

1 cup sugar   2 cups water
½ cup red cinnamon candies

Heat, stirring, until candies are dissolved.

Add some of

6 apples, pared, cored and sliced ¼-inch to ⅜-inch thick (just to cover bottom of pan)

Simmer gently until just tender; remove slices from syrup, drain and cool. Repeat until all apple slices are cooked. Arrange on baking sheet and freeze. Wrap slices in small packages as desired. Freeze syrup in small container.

FRENCH APPLE PIE
(8 servings)

Butter a 9-inch pie pan with

1 tablespoon butter

Sprinkle on

½ cup brown sugar   1 teaspoon cinnamon

Slice as thinly as possible

   Peeled, quartered, cored apples

Place the apples in a wheel design, covering the bottom of the pie plate. Then pile up as high as possible more thinly sliced apples. These do not need to be in a design.

Top the apples with

   1 tablespoon butter

Moisten the edge of the pie plate; cover with a very thin crust (recipe below). Freeze the pie. To serve set the frozen pie in a 450° oven; immediately reduce the temperature to 375°. (The high temperature makes the juice bubble up.) Bake 30 to 35 minutes. Invert immediately. Serve warm.

Crust:

Sift together

   1½ cups sifted flour   **½ teaspoon salt**

Cut in with pastry blender

   ½ cup shortening (use butter for special occasions)

until pieces are the size of small peas.

Add

   1 egg, lightly beaten

Sprinkle on

   2 tablespoons cold water one tablespoon at a time

Mix with fork. It will handle more easily if dough is chilled for half an hour. Roll out very thin on floured board.

BLUEBERRY PIE

OR STRAWBERRY, CURRANT, BLACKBERRY, RASPBERRY, ETC.

(8 servings)

Prepare pie crust (p. 126) for 9-inch pie plate.
Do not bake. Brush shell with egg white.

Filling:

Wash, separate and stem

   3 cups berries

Combine

| ⅔ to 1 cup sugar (or more) | 3½ tablespoons cornstarch |
| depending on acidity of fruit | 1½ tablespoons lemon juice |

Sprinkle over berries, stirring gently until well blended. Pour into un-baked pie crust. Dot with

   1 tablespoon butter

Let stand 15 minutes. Then cover with top crust. Trim the crust so that there is ¼-inch overhang. Wet edge of lower crust and seal crusts together by pinching dough. Freeze. To serve, bake unthawed pie at 450° for 15 to 20 minutes. (After first 10 minutes remove pie and cut vents in top crust.) Reduce temperature to 375° and bake 40 to 45 minutes longer. To freeze after baking bake at 450° for 10 minutes. Reduce to 350° and bake 30 minutes more or until crust is golden. Cool quickly and freeze. To serve, defrost and warm in 350° oven about 15 minutes.

CRANBERRY SAUCE
(1 quart)

Boil until sugar dissolves

| 2 cups water | 2 cups sugar |

Add

   1 pound cranberries (4 cups), rinsed

Cook over medium heat for 15 minutes after mixture boils. Cool quickly and freeze in quantities suitable for your family's use. Defrost to serve.

CRANBERRY ORANGE RELISH
(1 quart)

Put through food chopper

| 1 pound fresh cranberries | 2 oranges, quartered and seeded |

Add

  2 cups sugar

Mix well. Freeze in quantities suitable for your family's use. To serve, defrost.

FRUIT TORTE
(8 servings)

This begins with the blueberry season and goes through the peach and plum season on into apple time!

Cream

  1 cup sugar   ½ cup butter

Add

  1 cup flour, sifted   Salt
  1 teaspoon baking soda   2 eggs

Place in 9-inch spring form. Cover entire top surface with one of the following or a combination of:

  1 pint blueberries   Sliced peaches
  24 halved pitted Italian plums Sliced apples
     (also called prune plums),
     skin side up

Sprinkle top with

  Sugar   Flour (if fruit is very juicy)
  Lemon juice   Cinnamon (use a heavy hand)

Bake at 350° for 1 hour. Cool quickly and freeze. To serve, defrost. Best if served slightly warmed in 350° oven 10 minutes. Delicious with vanilla ice cream.

Miniature Fruit Tortes:

Bake as follows:

Fill miniature muffin tins with batter ⅔ way up the side.

Top each with some of

  2 pints blueberries (frozen or fresh)

Sprinkle with

Sugar   Cinnamon, big dash
Quick dash lemon juice

Bake at 350° 25 to 30 minutes. Remove and cool. Freeze. When ready to serve, place in miniature muffin papers. They are especially good slightly warmed.

MANGO SAUCE

If you have never tasted a mango, don't delay. Many supermarkets now carry them. They taste like a cross between a peach and an apricot, only better.

Peel, combine and cook until soft

6 cups mango slices   1½ cups water
  (from half-ripe mangos)

Add

1½ to 2 cups sugar

Cook for another 5 minutes. The amount of sugar will depend on the ripeness of the fruit. Freeze. To serve, defrost and serve sauce hot or cold with meat or as a dessert. It can also be served frozen, topped with

Whipped cream

PEACH CHUTNEY
(3 pints)

Of course you may can this, but since this is a freezer book why not freeze it? Then you won't have to sterilize the jars.

Combine

2 tablespoons salt   1 quart water

Pour over

7 cups sliced fresh peaches

Let stand 1 day. Drain.

Mix together and bring to boil

¼ cup cider vinegar   2 large cloves garlic
3 cups sugar

Add peaches. Cook about 45 minutes, until liquid is clear.

Remove peaches. Add

- 1 cup chopped onions
- 1 teaspoon ground ginger
- ¼ teaspoon crushed red pepper

¾ cup lime juice
1 cup raisins

Cook until a bit thickened, 12 to 15 minutes. Add

Peaches

½ cup chopped candied or
    preserved ginger

Bring to boil. Cool quickly and freeze in quantities suitable for your family's needs.

STEWED FRUITS

If you have any fruit trees and some of the fruit produced is bruised, do not discard it. Using the good slices you can make perfectly delicious stewed fruit which freezes well. It is good served with cooked meats, over ice cream or plain cake.

Boil for 3 minutes

2 cups water
½ to 1 cup sugar, depending on
    tartness of fruit

⅛ teaspoon salt

Drop into this boiling syrup

1 quart prepared fruit

Cook it gently until it is tender but not falling apart. You might like to add cinnamon to stewed peaches, apples or pears.

STRAWBERRY-RHUBARB PIE
(8 servings)

Prepare pie crust (p. 126) for 9-inch pie plate.
Do not bake. Brush shell with egg white.

Combine and place in unbaked shell

- 2 cups unpeeled, diced rhubarb
      stalks
- 2 cups sliced strawberries
- 3½ tablespoons cornstarch

1¼ to 2 cups sugar, depending
    on tartness of fruit
1 teaspoon orange rind
1 tablespoon butter

Permit them to stand for 15 minutes. Then cover with top crust. Trim the crust so that there is ¼-inch overhang. Wet edge of lower crust and seal crusts together by pinching dough. Freeze. To serve, bake unthawed pie at 450° for 15 to 20 minutes. After first 10 minutes, remove pie and cut vents in top crust. Reduce temperature to 375° and bake 40 to 45 minutes longer.

If you wish to bake and then freeze, bake at 450° for 10 minutes, reduce heat to 350° and bake 30 minutes more. Cool quickly and freeze. To serve, defrost. You may warm the pie at 350° for 15 minutes.

If after doing all of this baking, the day comes when the freezer is empty, you can replenish your supplies, utilizing all the wonderful frozen fruits you put away during the summer. Remember not to refreeze frozen fruits without first cooking or baking them.

4

The Unharried Hostess

The Unharried Hostess

USING YOUR FREEZER
IN PARTY PLANNING

Man's social instincts and his desire not to eat his sirloin in solitude have led him to be a great party goer and giver. It is his role as party giver that concerns us here, for if he, and his wife, wish to continue socializing they must take their turn as host and hostess, whether it be for a backyard barbecue or black-tie dinner. If you are one of those people who anticipate party-giving with nothing but dread, why not try our formula before forfeiting your entertaining to the local restaurant. There is nothing as gracious or warm as entertaining in your own home.

Once you do take the plunge and the invitations have been issued, it is too late to worry about how it will turn out. Anyway, it is far more sensible to spend your time planning your menus, shopping and cooking.

The key word in the previous paragraph, as you may have guessed, is *planning!* It will make the difference between enjoying your company and counting each moment until your guests depart. To borrow a line from our cookbook *Elegant But Easy,* "Entertaining really should be fun, for the hostess as well as her guests," and with today's freezers this is almost as easily done as said. All last-minute worries and most of the work can be eliminated since entire party menus can be frozen weeks ahead of time. At serving time the cook (YOU!) need not spend her time at the kitchen stove —she can wear her black satin sheath without fear of grease spots.

At cocktail parties and teas you will be able to mingle with your guests; at dinners and luncheons, sit down with them; and on weekends, stroll, make small talk and generally party!

On the following pages we have gone into detail about several types of entertaining from the relatively simple teas to the more complicated weekend house guests, for, with the possible exception of "The Man Who Came to Dinner," the latter can be the most demanding type of entertaining. If you are ready to give us a try, make out your guest lists, roll up your sleeves . . . and away we go!

Hors d'Oeuvres on the Rocks

The Cocktail Party

Are there many among you who would rather make a meal of hors d'oeuvres than anything else? Then be sure to entertain at cocktail parties! They lend themselves particularly well to "helpless" households without making the hostess kitchen-bound. They may be as seemingly casual as "do-drop-by-for-a-drink" or as formal as "to-meet-the-Smiths." They may consist of a few drinks and canapés or include a buffet supper. Whether simple or elaborate, they are wonderful for almost any occasion (with the exception of children's birthdays!). And above all they are perfect to write about in this book since so many hors d'oeuvres can be frozen.

Hot hors d'oeuvres are probably the most appealing but be sure to limit the oven-heated variety if you have no kitchen help. You can get around this problem with chafing dishes or those marvelous electrically heated glass trays. This is one sure method of cutting down on visits to the kitchen.

Choose your cold hors d'oeuvres as you would your guests; include only those which retain their good looks and good taste through several hours of cocktailing!

Be sure to keep your canapé trays as full as you keep your ash trays empty—in other words have enough! But you must be judicious about what "enough" is if the cocktails are before dinner. Keep the cocktail hour fairly short so that the guests will be able to see the dinner as well as do justice to it. Two or three hors d'oeuvres, depending on the number of guests, should be ample.

If the party is of several hours' duration, the sky's the limit. In any case, mix rather than match varieties.

No matter the type of cocktail party, hors d'oeuvres make the first impression, so give them some thought. Using your freezer will give you a great deal of thinking time since you can complete most of the cooking long before the invitations are even in the mail!

Hot Hors d'Oeuvres

BROILED JUMBO SHRIMP
(25 shrimp)

Shell and devein

25 jumbo shrimp

Marinate overnight in

2 cups French dressing

Freeze in marinade. To serve, defrost, drain and broil as close to heat as possible for 3 minutes on each side.

CHAFING DISH MEATBALLS AND FRANKS

Combine

  2 pounds ground chuck   1 large grated onion
  1 slightly beaten egg   Salt to taste

Mix and shape into 50 to 60 small balls. Drop into sauce of

  1 bottle chili sauce   Juice of 1 lemon
  ½ large jar grape jelly

Simmer until brown.

Add

  2 pounds frankfurters, sliced on the diagonal ½ inch thick

Cool and freeze. To serve, defrost and reheat slowly. Serve from chafing dish with cocktail picks.

Many people tell us they are so fond of the meatballs and sauce that they make larger balls and serve them in the sauce as a main course.

CHEESE CIGARETTES
(makes 60 to 70)

In a saucepan melt

  2½ tablespoons butter

Remove from heat and blend in

  3 tablespoons flour

Gradually add, stirring

  1½ cups milk   ¼ teaspoon salt

Return to heat and cook until thickened, stirring with wire whisk.

Slowly add

  ½ cup heavy cream

Season to taste with

Salt and pepper

While cream sauce is still hot add

½ pound freshly grated
  Parmesan cheese

2 egg yolks, beaten
¼ teaspoon cayenne pepper

Place in covered bowl in refrigerator. Let paste harden to spreading consistency. Remove crusts from

3 loaves very fresh white bread

Flatten each slice by rolling with rolling pin.

Spread each slice with paste and roll like cigarette.

Freeze. To serve, defrost and fry in deep hot fat at 475° until brown. Drain on paper towel and serve. Keep hot on electric tray.

CHEESE LOBSTER ROLLS
(70 to 80 rolls)

Melt in double boiler

¼ pound butter

½ pound pasteurized processed
  cheese

Add

1 pound lobster meat, fresh or frozen, cut in pieces

Remove crusts from

2 loaves very fresh sliced white bread

Roll very thin with rolling pin. Spread lobster mixture on bread slices. Roll up and freeze. When ready to serve, cut each roll in half and spread with

Melted butter

Defrost and bake at 400° for 10 to 15 minutes.

CHEESE SAVORIES
(5 dozen)

Put through food chopper

½ pound yellow cheese   1 onion
8 slices crisp bacon

Blend with

2 teaspoons mayonnaise   1 teaspoon dry mustard

Cut into 1½-inch rounds (you'll get two from each slice)

2 loaves thick fresh sliced white bread

Toast on one side. Spread mixture on other side. Freeze. To serve, defrost and broil 2 to 4 minutes.

CLAMS NORMANDE
(30 clams)

In a kettle with just enough water to cover bottom place

36 well-scrubbed large clams

Cover and steam until shells open. Remove the clams from the shells, discarding tough necks. Reserve 30 of the smallest shell halves.

Sauté for 1 minute

4 finely chopped shallots or   6 tablespoons finely chopped
   scallions   mushrooms

in

2 tablespoons butter

Place the clams, shallots, mushrooms and

1½ tablespoons chives   1 teaspoon parsley

in grinder and grind with finest blade or chop very finely.

Combine with

2 tablespoons bread crumbs   1 tablespoon sherry

Mix well. Add more sherry, if necessary, to moisten well. Heap the mixture into the reserved half shells. Freeze. To serve, defrost, sprinkle with

Buttered bread crumbs   Paprika

Bake at 350° for about 15 minutes, until crumbs are golden.

COCKTAIL MEDALLIONS
(Makes about 4½ dozen)

Drain syrup from

  1 #2 can pineapple chunks

Stir in

  3 tablespoons soy sauce   ¼ teaspoon ginger
  1 tablespoon wine vinegar   ¼ teaspoon salt
  1 tablespoon brown sugar

Count the pineapple chunks and add to marinade.

Cut in half

  1 pound chicken livers (about 30)

so that there is a number equal to number of pineapple chunks. Drain

  2 5-ounce cans water chestnuts

and cut into same number of pieces. Add livers and water chestnuts to marinade. Cover and refrigerate several hours. Cut

  30 bacon strips in half lengthwise

Using a small wooden skewer for each medallion, skewer one end of bacon strip; then add a piece of pineapple, piece of liver and piece of water chestnut. Wrap other end of bacon around, skewering it to hold. Place all medallions in flat freezer container and pour marinade over them. Freeze. To serve, defrost, drain marinade and reserve and arrange on broiler pan. Broil about 4 inches from heat, turning once, until livers are done and bacon is crisp, 4 to 5 minutes. Brush once or twice with marinade. Keep hot on hot tray or in chafing dish.

FRANKS 'N' KRAUT
(3 dozen)

Very hearty—almost a supper in itself.

Parboil for 5 minutes

  12 large-size all-beef franks

Simmer 15 minutes

  1 pound sauerkraut   3 tablespoons brown sugar
  2 tablespoons caraway seeds   Shallot plugged with cloves

Roll very thin

   18 slices white bread, crusts removed

Spread each slice with

   Mustard

Place on each

   1 frank, trimmed to bread size   Hot sauerkraut

Roll up and freeze. When ready to serve, defrost, cut in half and bake at 400° for about 30 minutes.

FRANKS IN SOUR CREAM

Cut into ½-inch diagonal slices

   12 franks

Brown them in

   2 tablespoons hot oil

Stir in

2 tablespoons flour	¼ teaspoon salt
3 tablespoons chili sauce	¼ cup water
1 cup sour cream	1 tablespoon caraway seeds
2 teaspoons sugar	

Freeze. To serve, defrost and heat to boiling. Serve from chafing dish with cocktail picks.

LITTLE ROCK CANAPÉS

Sauté until tender

   1 medium bunch green onions (scallions)   ½ cup butter
     and tops, cut medium fine

Add

2 packages frozen chopped spinach, barely cooked and drained	¼ teaspoon garlic powder Salt and pepper to taste Few drops either hot pepper
8 ounces crabmeat, fresh or canned, cut fine	sauce or Tabasco Fresh chopped parsley (optional)
1 3-ounce jar grated Parmesan cheese	

Combine thoroughly. Freeze. To serve, defrost and heat to serve with

   Crackers or corn chips

OLIVE CHEESE BALLS
(About 4 dozen)

Blend in mixer

2 cups finely shredded sharp   ½ cup softened butter
Cheddar cheese

Add

1 cup flour   1 teaspoon paprika

Combine thoroughly. Shape 1 tablespoon of this mixture around each of

48 large pimiento-stuffed olives

Keep dipping your hands in flour to prevent sticking. Freeze. To serve,
bake frozen balls at 400° for 20 minutes or until golden.

Variations:

The cheese mixture may also be wrapped around tiny browned sausage
balls or small slices of uncooked frankfurters.

QUICHE LORRAINE, MINIATURE
(60 tarts)

Follow pastry and custard recipes under Quiche Lorraine on page 184.

After rolling out pastry dough, cut rounds 1¾ inches in diameter and
fit into miniature muffin tins.

Crumble

8 slices bacon

Place a piece of bacon in each dough-filled tin. Fill tarts with custard.
Freeze. To serve, defrost and bake at 425° for 5 minutes. Reduce heat to
325° and bake 12 minutes longer, until custard is puffed and brown.
Serve in miniature muffin paper cups.

ROLLED PANCAKE BITES
(40 pancakes)

Make dollar-size pancakes according to package directions, using a thin batter.

Combine

2 tablespoons mayonnaise
3-ounce package softened cream cheese

4 teaspoons horseradish
2 large cans deviled ham

Fill the pancakes with this mixture; roll and secure with toothpicks. Freeze. To serve, defrost and broil for two minutes under broiler or sauté lightly in

Butter

in skillet or chafing dish.

RUMAKI BALLS
(Makes about 9 dozen)

Combine and mix well

3 pounds chicken livers, cooked and chopped fine
6 eggs, hard-cooked and chopped fine
1 cup minced onion

1 8-ounce can water chestnuts, drained and chopped fine
Salt to taste
1 pound crisp cooked bacon, chopped fine

Add enough of

½ cup mayonnaise

to hold ingredients together. Cover; chill several hours or overnight. Shape into small balls about ¾ inch in diameter. Roll in

Flavored bread crumbs

Freeze. To serve, defrost and sauté in

Salad oil

until balls are golden brown, turning once carefully.

Keep hot in chafing dish or on hot tray. Serve with cocktail picks.

SATÉ
SPICY PORK DISH

(We often use this as a main dish for family dinner.)

Combine

¼ cup creamy peanut butter
1½ teaspoons ground coriander
1½ teaspoons salt
½ teaspoon red-pepper flakes
1 teaspoon ground cumin

¾ cup grated onion
1 clove garlic, finely chopped
1½ tablespoons lemon juice
1 tablespoon brown sugar
3 tablespoons soy sauce

Add and toss until well-coated

2 pounds boneless pork cubes

Refrigerate in marinade overnight. Freeze in marinade. When ready to serve, defrost, drain and reserve marinade; place pork cubes in broiler pan about 4 inches from heat and broil 10 minutes, turning after 5 minutes. Baste several times with marinade. Reduce heat to 475° and heat 20 minutes longer. Serve from chafing dish.

SAUSAGE BALLS IN PASTRY BLANKETS
(65 balls)

Combine

1 pound sausage meat
2 teaspoons curry powder

½ teaspoon nutmeg
¼ teaspoon powdered sage

Form into small balls about ½ tablespoon each. Fry out some of the fat and drain balls on absorbent paper. Prepare cheese pastry by blending

½ pound sharp cheese
½ cup soft butter
1½ cups sifted flour

¼ teaspoon salt
1 teaspoon paprika

Shape 1 tablespoon dough around each sausage ball. Freeze. To serve, place unthawed balls on ungreased baking sheet. Bake at 400° for 12 to 15 minutes.

SMITHFIELD HAM IN BISCUITS
(150 biscuits)

Baking Powder Biscuits:

Sift together

4 cups flour, sifted   1 teaspoon salt
2 tablespoons baking powder

Cut in until mixture resembles coarse crumbs

½ cup cold butter   ½ cup shortening

Add

1½ cups milk

*Roll out ½ inch thick. Cut out jigger-sized rounds. Partially bake at 400°
for 7 minutes. Split and butter. Fill with*

Paper-thin slices of Smithfield ham

or

Spread with mixture of

2 jars Smithfield-ham spread   ½ that amount of mayonnaise

Freeze. To serve heat at 400° for about 7 minutes, without defrosting.

STUFFED MUSHROOM CAPS
(35 mushrooms)

Clean and remove stems from

35 medium mushrooms

Sauté stems with

¼ pound butter   1 large onion

Add

½ package prepared-stuffing mix   Salt and pepper to taste
1 cup chicken bouillon   Garlic salt to taste
   (made with 1 cube)

Stuff caps with mixture. In 10 x 15-inch pan melt

¼ pound butter

Place mushrooms in pan. Bake at 350° for 10 minutes. Cool. Cover with
foil. Freeze. To serve, bake unthawed at 350° for 15 minutes, covered.
Remove foil, broil 3 to 5 minutes.

Additional Suggestions for Hot Hors d'Oeuvres:

Cheese Boereg (p. 64)
Crêpes filled with Crabmeat (p. 91)
Shelby's Cheese Sticks (p. 104)
Potato Puffs Parmesan (p. 57)
Pastry Snails (p. 100)
Cream Puffs filled with Cream Cheese and Ham (p. 98)
Cream Puffs filled with Cream Cheese and Roquefort (p. 98)
Tempura (p. 69)
Garlic Shoestrings (p. 171)

Cold Hors d'Oeuvres

BLEU-CRAB DUNK

Mix together in order given

½ cup bleu cheese	1 clove garlic, minced
⅓ cup softened cream cheese	1 teaspoon lemon juice
2 tablespoons mayonnaise	6 ounces crabmeat
½ teaspoon Worcestershire sauce	

Freeze. To serve, defrost and serve in bowl surrounded with

Potato chips

CHEDDAR ROQUEFORT ROLL

Grate

¼ pound sharp Cheddar cheese

Mix thoroughly with

3 ounces softened cream cheese	¼ pound Roquefort cheese

Add, mixing well

2 tablespoons onion juice	¼ teaspoon Tabasco
1 teaspoon mayonnaise	

Form into cylinders about 1 inch in diameter. Roll on waxed paper that is covered with

Paprika

Freeze. To serve, defrost, slice and serve with

Rye rounds or crackers

LIPTAUER CHEESE
(4 small crocks, 8 cups)

Mix together

4 pounds softened cream cheese
2 pounds softened unsalted butter
2 tablespoons caraway seeds

2 tablespoons chopped chives
2 tablespoons chopped capers
4 teaspoons paprika

Freeze in crocks or plastic containers. Thaw at room temperature about 4 or 5 hours. Serve with

Thinly sliced pumpernickel

(If possible buy the variety of pumpernickel that comes in small rolls, wrapped in aluminum foil, available in gourmet food shops.)

A crock or two of this cheese and some rolls of pumpernickel make a delicious and attractive gift.

TIPSY CHEESE SPREAD

This is not as daring as it sounds, but very delicious.

Place small portions of the following ingredients in blender and blend thoroughly. Repeat until all is blended.

½ pound sharp Cheddar cheese,
    room temperature
¼ pound Swiss cheese,
    room temperature
¼ pound cream cheese, softened
¼ pound pecan meats

1 large onion
¼ cup finely chopped parsley
Dash tabasco
¼ teaspoon salt
¼ cup gin

Mix well and add

⅛ teaspoon dried tarragon

Freeze. To serve, defrost and serve with

Crackers   Rye rounds

WINE NUT ROLLS
(4 rolls)

Blend thoroughly

- 2 cups shredded sharp Cheddar cheese
- ½ pound bleu cheese
- 6 ounces cream cheese

Add

- 4 tablespoons red port wine
- ½ cup finely chopped walnuts
- 1 teaspoon grated onion
- 4 tablespoons finely chopped parsley
- Dash cayenne pepper

Chill until firm enough to shape into rolls about 1¼ inches in diameter. Freeze. When ready to serve defrost in refrigerator. Slice and serve with

Crackers

Additional Suggestions for Cold Hors d'Oeuvres:

See particularly the section on tea parties for cold canapés equally suitable for cocktail parties (p. 189).

Spreads (pp. 191-193):

Almond Olive
Avocado
Chicken and Bacon
Cognac Cheese
Crabmeat

Ham Horseradish
Toasted Pecan
Orange Cheese
Variety of Butter Spreads

BLACK TIE OR BLUE DENIM

Dinner Parties Both Formal and Informal

The story is told of a Chicago hostess who gave her cook a black dress uniform for Christmas. Cook was so incensed that she reportedly served the holiday bird stuffed with said uniform and a note reading, "I quit."

Such situations seldom arise these days since there are few cooks around to give presents to, but you, as mistress of a household, still must entertain dinner guests as well as serve family meals. Though you are probably your own cook you do have a new variety of "faithful old family retainer"—your freezer. To take advantage of this silent servant for dinner parties, advance planning and cooking are essential.

If possible allow yourself plenty of time for leisurely cooking, and do not undertake to feed more people than you can handle comfortably for serving and seating. It is far more satisfactory (for the nerves particularly) to give a series of two or three small dinner parties, repeating your menu each time. If you have been reading this book attentively, you will cook each dish in quantity, dividing and freezing it in portions suitable to the size of each party.

The formality or informality of the occasion will dictate your menu. Though several courses are served at a sit-down dinner, a main course of several dishes and dessert are appropriate for a buffet. Sit-down dinners usually require an extra pair of hands to serve, but if you plan your menu wisely you can perform maid-duty without being last-minute kitchen slave and jack-in-the-box. Buffet service is perfect for less formal entertaining and for large groups. Plan your buffet table with an eye for color, ease of service and overall effect. If laps are to be used as tables serve only foods that do not require a knife. It is, however, far more satisfactory for guests, sofas and carpets to provide snack tables or small tables that will seat four to six. Above all, your choice of menu and type of service should suit your own taste, home and budget.

Whether you are entertaining after a football game or before a dance, for a new arrival in town or departing friends, or just because you like to entertain, make your work as easy as possible by relying for most of your menu on freezable dishes. The day of your party should find you performing only such chores as table setting, flower arranging and food heating—no real cooking. Even such unfreezables as aspics and salads can certainly be prepared a day or two in advance and refrigerated until serving time.

The question we are most frequently asked is "Do you really take a nap the day of a dinner party?" (referring to a line we wrote in *Elegant but Easy*). The answer is most assuredly "Yes" and you can do the same by following these suggestions and menus.

Sit-down Dinners 1

HORS D'OEUVRES	Rumaki Balls (p. 146)
	Liptauer Cheese Spread (p. 150)
FIRST COURSE	*Cream of Mushroom Soup
MAIN COURSE	*Lobster à l'Américaine
	*Orange Rice Ring
	Peas Suprême (p. 57)
	Grapefruit Avocado Freeze (p. 179)
	Caraway Cheese Bread (p. 41)
	White Wine
DESSERT	Crêpes Suzette (p. 92)
	Demitasse

CREAM OF MUSHROOM SOUP
(8 servings)

Excellent to make from stems if you stuff caps for hors d'oeuvres.

Slice

   1½ pounds fresh mushrooms

Sauté for 5 minutes in

   3 tablespoons butter

Sprinkle with

   3 tablespoon flour

Stir and cook one minute. Remove from heat and add

   1 cup chicken stock

Stir well and add

   7 more cups stock

Simmer 10 minutes. Add

   ¾ cup heavy cream

Cool quickly and freeze. To serve, defrost just enough to remove from container and heat very slowly over direct heat (watch carefully) or over hot water.

LOBSTER À L'AMERICAINE
(8 servings)

Cut into bite-sized pieces

   4 pounds cooked lobster meat

Sprinkle with

   2 teaspoons salt

Fry lobster until it starts to brown in

   1 cup salad oil

Add

2 small onions, diced	1 8-ounce can tomato paste
2 cloves garlic, minced	Equal amount water

Warm and ignite

⅔ cup brandy

When flame dies down add to lobster with

1½ cups dry white wine

Add

1 teaspoon chervil	Few grains cayenne pepper
2 sprigs parsley, chopped	

Cool quickly and freeze. To serve, defrost and reheat very slowly in top of double boiler.

ORANGE RICE RING
(10 to 12 servings)

Melt in dish that you will use for baking

¼ pound butter

Combine

1 box long-grain rice, cooked and drained	½ cup sugar
5 eggs, beaten	1 cup orange juice

Combine with the butter and mix well. Bake at 350° for 30 minutes. Freeze. To serve, defrost and bake 30 minutes more.

Menu 2

HORS D'OEUVRES	Chafing-Dish Meatballs and Franks (p. 140)
	Tipsy Cheese Spread (p. 150)
MAIN COURSE	*Chicken with Lemon Cream
	*Asparagus Polonaise
	Boulghour Pilaf (p. 224)
	Honeybuns (p. 214)
	White Wine or Rosé
DESSERT	Orange Soufflé (p. 207)

CHICKEN WITH LEMON CREAM
(8 servings)

Melt in heavy skillet

¼ cup butter

Brown in the butter

2 broilers, cut in serving pieces

Cover skillet and cook over medium heat for 5 minutes. Remove chicken and add to skillet

3 tablespoons dry sherry
3 tablespoons dry white wine
Grated peel of 1 orange

2 tablespoons lemon juice
Salt and pepper to taste
1½ cups heavy or medium cream

Boil quickly, stirring, and pour over chicken which has been placed in shallow casserole. Freeze. To serve, defrost and sprinkle with

¾ cup finely grated Swiss cheese

Arrange on top

8 wafer-thin slices of lemon

Heat in 350° oven for 30 to 40 minutes and run under broiler for a few minutes to brown cheese.

ASPARAGUS POLONAISE
(6 servings)

Cook and drain

2 packages frozen asparagus

Melt

¼ cup sweet butter

When butter foams stir in

2 tablespoons soft bread crumbs

Continue to cook over low heat until crumbs are browned. Remove from fire and stir in

1 small hard-cooked egg,
chopped fine

½ tablespoon finely chopped
parsley
Salt and pepper to taste

Pour over the cooked asparagus.

Menu 3

HORS D'OEUVRES	Quiche Lorraine, Miniature (p. 145)
	Cocktail Medallions (p. 143)
FIRST COURSE	*Gazpacho à la Sanjuan
MAIN COURSE	*Coulibiac
	Artichokes and Mushrooms (p. 53)
	White Wine
SALAD COURSE	*Green Salad with Oil and Wine Vinegar
	Dressing
	Cheeses
DESSERT	*Mousse à la Maison Blanche
	Demitasse

GAZPACHO À LA SANJUAN
(8 servings)

In mixing bowl place

¾ cup olive oil
4 cloves crushed garlic
½ medium onion, crushed against
side of bowl

4 or 5 snips fresh parsley,
crushed against side of bowl
1½ teaspoons salt
½ cup vinegar
Some of 1 cup red Burgundy

Place half this base in blender. Make soup in 2 batches. Fill blender two-thirds full with half of

2 ripe tomatoes
1 16-ounce can whole tomatoes

1 24-ounce can tomato juice
1 large, ripe avocado

Blend at top speed for about 2 minutes. Pour into bowl and place remaining ingredients in blender. Blend about 2 minutes and combine with first batch. Strain mixture through fine wire strainer. Press any residue left in strainer against sides with spoon until only a wet pulp remains in strainer; discard. Freeze. Defrost to serve.

If the soup is not salty enough add and stir well

¼ teaspoon salt

Top with

Snips of chive, fresh or frozen

Serve very well chilled.

COULIBIAC
(8 servings)

We will not attempt to conceal the all too obvious fact that this incomparable dish requires a lot of preparation, but you will note that it can be done in as many as five stages, each stage being frozen until the final assembling. We guarantee that your reputation as a gourmet is a certainty once you serve this.

Make brioche dough according to the recipe on page 110. Follow the directions to the point where you put the dough in the refrigerator or freezer.

Fish Stock:

Ask your fish market for 1 pound heads, skin and bones from sole, salmon or flounder. Put in kettle

1 small onion, finely sliced	3 peppercorns
1 piece celery	1 teaspoon salt
½ leek	½ cup dry white wine
¼ carrot	1½ cups water
1 small bay leaf, broken in half	

Bring to a boil. Add fish scraps. Cover and simmer 25 to 30 minutes. Strain fish stock. It may be frozen at this point. To use, defrost.

Panade:

Melt

    ¼ cup butter

Take from heat and stir in

½ cup flour	⅛ teaspoon nutmeg
⅛ teaspoon cayenne pepper	1 raw egg
½ teaspoon salt	1 cup strained fish stock

Stir over fire until it comes away clean from sides of pan. Place on flat plate and chill or freeze. To use after freezing, defrost in refrigerator.

Crumb Mixture:

Combine

1 cup fresh bread crumbs	½ teaspoon cardamom seed
2 teaspoons dry mustard	½ cup melted butter
1 teaspoon salt	
1 teaspoon freshly cracked white pepper	

Add

½ cup freshly grated Parmesan cheese

Refrigerate or freeze. To use after freezing, defrost at room temperature.

Onions:

Combine and cook until soft

4 finely chopped onions   2 tablespoons butter

Freeze if desired or refrigerate. To use after freezing, defrost at room temperature.

To Assemble Coulibiac:

Roll out chilled brioche dough on well-floured board in ¼-inch thick oval. Brush entire surface with

Cooled, melted butter

Sprinkle with

Crumb mixture

Leave ¼-inch margin all around. Scatter over top

1½ pounds lobster meat, cooked and flaked

Dab over fish

Panade

Drop by tablespoonful over fish

1 pint sour cream

Sprinkle with

½ cup freshly grated Parmesan   4 hard-cooked eggs, chopped
cheese   Onion mixture
1 sprig dill, minced

Flour your hands and roll up like jelly roll. Place it on a buttered jelly-roll pan. Shape like large crescent. Cover with cloth and let rise in warm place for 30 minutes. Brush with

Beaten egg

Bake at 425° for 20 minutes, cool and freeze. To serve, defrost and bake at 350° for about 30 minutes. You may also refrigerate it, unbaked, overnight and bake it at 400° for 30 to 40 minutes.

SALAD AND CHEESES

Even though the salad does not freeze, you can prepare the greens in the morning and refrigerate in a plastic bag until serving time. The dressing may be prepared a few days ahead.

Use

Lettuce	Endive
Romaine	Escarole

The cheeses may be

Brie	Grape
Camembert	Roquefort, etc.
Cheshire	

MOUSSE À LA MAISON BLANCHE
(8 servings)

In top of double boiler melt

2 squares bitter chocolate

Stir in

½ cup confectioners' sugar   1 cup warm milk

Cook, stirring until it boils. Remove from heat and stir in

1 envelope unflavored gelatin
   softened in
3 tablespoons cold water

Add

¾ cup granulated sugar   ¼ teaspoon salt
1 teaspoon vanilla

Chill until slightly thick. Then beat until light. Whip until stiff

1 pint heavy cream

Fold into chocolate mixture. Pour into 1½ quart mold and freeze. When ready to serve, defrost in refrigerator, unmold and garnish with

Shaved semisweet chocolate

Sit-down Buffet 1

HORS D'OEUVRES   Cheddar Roquefort Roll (p. 149)

Clams Normande (p. 142)

MAIN COURSE   *Cannelloni

Frozen Zucchini

Salad or Aspic

Onion French Bread (p. 173)

Red Wine

DESSERT   *Viennese Torte

Coffee

CANNELLONI
(12 servings)

Cook until almost tender

2 pounds wide lasagna noodles

If you wish you may add green food coloring to the boiling water to make Cannelloni Verdi (Green Cannelloni). Drain noodles and lay them on damp towels. Cut each strip in half crosswise.

Filling:

Combine and blend thoroughly

2 pounds ricotta cheese	2 garlic cloves, minced
2 cups freshly grated Parmesan	4 eggs
2 cups ground cooked ham	Salt and pepper to taste
½ cup minced parsley	

Put 1 tablespoon of filling into center of each rectangle and roll up like jelly roll. Lay the cannelloni side by side in buttered baking dishes, brush with

Melted butter

On one side of noodles pour in the Tomato Meat Sauce; on the other side pour in the béchamel sauce. Freeze. To serve, defrost, sprinkle noodles generously with

Grated Parmesan cheese

Sprinkle béchamel sauce with

  Pinch of grated nutmeg

Bake at 375° for 20 to 30 minutes.

Tomato Meat Sauce:

In large heavy saucepan heat

  ½ cup butter   ½ cup olive oil

In it sauté until soft

  2 onions, minced   2 stalks celery, minced
  2 cloves garlic, minced

Add

  1½ pounds ground beef   1 pound ground veal

Brown lightly. Stir in

  2 2-pound cans Italian plum tomatoes

Add

  Salt and freshly ground pepper   Oregano
     to taste

Bring to a boil. Cover and simmer very slowly, stirring occasionally, for two to three hours. Remove cover for last hour of cooking. When sauce is done, skim fat from surface.

Béchamel Sauce:

In a heavy saucepan melt

  6 tablespoons butter

In it cook until soft

  2 tablespoons finely chopped onion

Take from heat and stir in

  ½ cup flour

Return to heat and cook slowly, stirring, until it begins to turn golden. Remove from heat; gradually add

  4 cups scalded milk

Return to heat, cook, stirring vigorously with wire whisk, until smooth and thickened. Add

½ teaspoon or more salt   2 sprigs parsley
White pepper, to taste

Cook slowly, stirring frequently, for about 30 minutes, or until sauce is reduced by one-third. Strain.

VIENNESE CHOCOLATE TORTE
(12 servings)

In top of double boiler melt

1 6-ounce package semisweet   ¼ cup coffee
   chocolate pieces

Stir to blend and cool. Grease 8-inch spring form. Line bottom with waxed paper and grease the paper. Beat until soft peaks form, about 10 minutes.

6 eggs   ⅔ cup sugar

Fold cooled chocolate mixture into egg mixture. Sift, 1 tablespoon at a time, over batter

⅔ cup sifted flour

Fold each addition into batter. Pour batter into pan. Bake 55 to 60 minutes at 300° F. Cool 10 minutes on wire rack; remove sides of pan. Cool cake completely. Remove cake and turn upside down. Split cake in half.

Spread bottom half with

¾ cup apricot preserves

Replace top. Spread top with another

¾ cup apricot preserves

Chill. Pour glaze over cake while glaze is still hot. Cover tops and sides. Freeze. To serve, defrost, unwrapped.

Glaze:

Melt in top of double boiler

1 package semisweet chocolate   3 tablespoons light corn syrup
   bits   2 teaspoons coffee

Menu 2

HORS D'OEUVRES	Rolled Pancake Bites (p. 145)
	Stuffed Mushroom Caps (p. 148)
MAIN COURSE	*Chicken Amandine
	Walnut Broccoli (p. 58)
	*Cheesey Baked Potatoes
	*Cranberry Nut Rolls
	Peach Chutney (p. 131)
	White Wine or Rosé
DESSERT	*Cocoa Roll
	Coffee

CHICKEN AMANDINE
(15 to 20 servings)

Quarter

  5 2½- to 3-pound broilers

Season with

  Salt and pepper

Dredge lightly in

  Flour

Brown chicken pieces on both sides in

  1½ cups butter

Pour over the browned chicken pieces

  ¼ cup dry sherry or brandy

Remove chicken from the pan and add to pan juices

  2 tablespoons butter   1 tablespoon finely chopped
                                              shallots

Cook for 1 minute. Add

  1 cup blanched slivered almonds

Brown slowly. Remove from heat and stir in

  1 tablespoon tomato paste   3 tablespoons flour
  1 teaspoon meat glaze

Add gradually, stirring

  3 cups chicken stock   ½ cup white wine

Return to heat, bring to a boil. Season to taste with

  Salt and pepper

Return chicken to sauce. Add

  2 sprigs fresh tarragon
              or
  2 teaspoons dried tarragon

Cool quickly and freeze. To serve, defrost, adjust seasonings and simmer for 35 minutes in covered pan. Arrange on serving platter and sprinkle with

  1 cup almonds, blanched, slivered and browned in butter

CHEESEY BAKED POTATOES
(16 servings)

Bake

  16 medium baking potatoes

*When cool, split in half and scoop out pulp. Mash potato well **and** combine with*

  4 slightly beaten eggs   4 tablespoons minced onion
  ¼ pound melted butter   Salt and pepper to taste
  16 slices of slightly melted
      sharp Cheddar cheese

Fill potato skins and freeze. To serve, defrost and reheat at 350° for 30 minutes.

CRANBERRY NUT ROLLS
(20 rolls)

Grease generously 20 miniature muffin tins. Divide over tins

  ¼ cup chopped nuts

Crush together

  ½ cup whole cranberry sauce
  ¼ cup brown sugar

Divide mixture over muffin tins. Press into each tin

½ refrigerator biscuit shaped like crescent

Bake at 400° for 10 minutes. Invert pans to remove biscuits. Cool and freeze. To serve, defrost and bake 8 to 10 minutes in muffin papers in tins at 350°.

COCOA ROLL
(8 servings—Duplicate for large party)

In large mixing bowl beat until stiff

6 eggs whites

Fold in

6 beaten egg yolks

Sift together, then fold in

1 cup sugar	¼ teaspoon baking powder
4 tablespoons cocoa	½ teaspoon salt
4 tablespoons flour	

Fold in

1 teaspoon vanilla

Place in 10 x 15-inch jelly-roll pan which has been lined with greased waxed paper. Bake at 350° for 12 to 15 minutes. Cool 5 minutes and turn out onto towel sprinkled with

Confectioners' sugar

Roll-up on long side. Cool; unroll and when thoroughly cool fill with

½ pint heavy cream, whipped	½ teaspoon peppermint extract
1 tablespoon confectioners' sugar	

Roll up again on long side. Freeze. Defrost to serve. Cover with icing.

Icing:

Blend until smooth

1 cup confectioners' sugar	2 tablespoons hot coffee
3 tablespoons cocoa	½ teaspoon vanilla
2 tablespoons melted butter	¼ teaspoon salt

Buffets 1

HORS D'OEUVRES   Broiled Jumbo Shrimp (p. 139)
                              Rumaki Balls (p. 146)

MAIN COURSE   *Beef Stroganoff
                              *Gnocchi alla Romana
                              Salad
                              Baked Asparagus (p. 53)

DESSERT   *Mousse au Chocolat

BEEF STROGANOFF
(10 servings)

Cut into 2 x ¼ x ¼-inch strips

  4 pounds boneless beef (tenderloin, sirloin, rib)

Dredge meat with following mixture

  1 cup flour
  2 teaspoons salt

  1 teaspoon monosodium
    glutamate
  ¼ teaspoon pepper

Heat in skillet

  ⅔ cup butter

Brown meat on all sides with

  1 cup finely chopped onion

Add

  3 10½-ounce cans beef bouillon

Cover and simmer 20 minutes. Combine and sauté

  1 pound sliced mushrooms

  6 tablespoons butter

Add to meat. Blend

  2 cups sour cream
  6 tablespoons tomato paste

  2 teaspoons Worcestershire
    sauce

Remove meat from heat and add sour cream mixture in small amounts. Cool quickly and freeze. When ready to serve, defrost and heat very slowly, stirring over low heat to prevent separation. Serve with

Gnocchi

The dish may also be heated in 350° oven for 30 minutes. Stir occasionally.

GNOCCHI ALLA ROMANA

Bring to a boil

1½ cups milk   1½ cups water

Gradually stir in

1 cup farina   1½ teaspoons salt

Cook over medium heat until thick, stirring. Remove from heat and beat in

¼ cup butter   ½ cup freshly grated Parmesan
3 eggs   cheese

Mix well and spread about ¼ inch thick on jelly-roll pan. Cool thoroughly and cut in shapes desired with a cookie cutter or cut into diamond shapes. Arrange in buttered baking dish in overlapping layers. Sprinkle with

1½ cups freshly grated Parmesan   ¼ cup butter
    cheese

Freeze. To serve, defrost and bake at 350° for about 30 minutes, or until golden and crisp.

MOUSSE AU CHOCOLAT
(6 to 8 servings)

How can anything so elegant be so simple!

In top of double boiler over hot water melt

½ pound excellent sweet   3 tablespoons water
    chocolate   ¼ cup sugar

Mix well, remove and cool. Add, 1 at a time, mixing well after each addition

4 egg yolks

Add

  1 inch vanilla-bean seeds

Fold in

  4 stiffly beaten egg whites

Spoon into individual dishes. Freeze. To serve, defrost in refrigerator.
Top with

  1 cup heavy cream, whipped

Menu 2

HORS D'OEUVRES	Wine Nut Rolls
	Sausage Balls in Pastry (p. 147)
MAIN COURSE	*Shrimp on a Green Bed
	*Carrot Cake
	*Garlic Shoestrings
	*Red-and-White Mold
DESSERT	*Chocolate Cheesecake
	Coffee

SHRIMP ON A GREEN BED
(10 servings)

In large skillet melt

  ½ cup butter

Add

½ pound fresh spinach, washed, drained and cut up	6 scallions, finely chopped
½ head Boston lettuce, cleaned and shredded	½ cup chopped parsley
	1½ ribs celery, finely chopped

Cover and simmer about 10 minutes. Add

½ cup bread crumbs	⅛ teaspoon freshly ground
1 teaspoon salt	black pepper
	¼ teaspoon mace

Spread mixture in bottom of shallow greased 3-quart casserole. Cover this mixture with

2 pounds peeled, uncooked shrimp

Melt

¼ cup butter

Remove from heat and blend in

4 tablespoons flour

Add slowly

2 cups light cream   2 cups milk

Return to heat and bring to boil, stirring. Simmer two minutes. Stir in

¼ cup freshly grated Parmesan   Salt and pepper to taste
   cheese

Pour sauce over shrimp. Sprinkle with

¼ cup buttered bread crumbs

Cool quickly and freeze. Defrost and bake at 350° for 45 minutes.

CARROT CAKE
(8 servings)

Mix thoroughly in bowl

1 cup shortening   1 tablespoon vanilla
½ cup dark brown sugar   2 beaten egg yolks
1 teaspoon salt   1¼ cups sifted flour
1 tablespoon cold water   1 cup cooked mashed carrots
1 tablespoon lemon juice   (or 2 jars baby-food carrots)

Add

½ teaspoon baking powder   ½ teaspoon baking soda

Fold in

2 stiffly beaten egg whites

Bake in greased 2-quart ring mold at 350° for 45 minutes. Cool quickly and freeze. To serve, defrost and bake at 350° for 15 to 25 minutes. Unmold. Center may be filled with vegetables.

GARLIC SHOESTRINGS

Brush

Slices of party rye

with

Melted butter

Sprinkle with

Garlic salt

Cut into thin strips. Freeze. To serve, toast unthawed at 400° for 5 minutes.

RED-AND-WHITE MOLD
(8 servings)

Stir

2 tablespoons lemon juice

into

2 cups whole cranberry sauce (1-pound can)

Pour into decorative mold and place in freezer. Meanwhile combine

1 cup heavy cream, whipped ¾ cup chopped nutmeats
¼ cup powdered sugar 2 teaspoons grated orange rind
1 teaspoon vanilla

Spoon this mixture over cranberry layer. Freeze. To serve, run knife around edge of mold, dip quickly in hot water and unmold on greens.

CHOCOLATE CHEESECAKE
(12 servings)

Lightly butter bottom and sides of 9-inch spring form. Mix together

1½ cups zwieback crumbs 2 tablespoons sugar
⅓ cup melted butter

Press into sides and bottom of pan. Melt over hot water

8 ounces sweet cooking chocolate

Remove from heat and cool slightly. Mix together

1¼ pounds cream cheese, 1½ teaspoons vanilla
softened 5 tablespoons sugar
¼ teaspoon salt

Beat in

  4 egg yolks

Fold in chocolate. Beat until stiff

  4 egg whites

Beat into whites, 1 tablespoon at a time, until firm

  5 tablespoons sugar

Whip until stiff

  1 cup heavy cream

Pour over egg-white mixture. Add the cream-cheese mixture. Sprinkle on the top

  ½ cup flour

Fold all ingredients together gently. Pour mixture into pan and bake at 325° for 1¼ hours. Turn off oven and allow cake to remain in oven 3 to 4 hours, even overnight. The cake may crack but that won't affect its delicious flavor. Chill cake. Remove the spring form. Freeze. To serve, defrost and top with

  1 cup heavy cream, whipped

Decorate cake with

  1 square unsweetened chocolate, shaved

Sunday Night Supper

HORS D'OEUVRES	Olive Cheese Balls (p. 145)
	Bleu Crab Dunk (p. 149)
MAIN COURSE	*Italian Macaroni Casserole
	*Onion French Bread
	Salad
DESSERT	Strawberry-Rhubarb Pie (p. 132)
	Coffee

ITALIAN MACARONI CASSEROLE
(12 servings)

Meat Filling:

Sauté in large skillet

  2 pounds ground beef   1 clove garlic
  2 medium onions, chopped

Add

1 8-ounce can tomato sauce	1½ teaspoons oregano
1 6-ounce can tomato paste	1½ teaspoons salt
1 4-ounce can sliced mushrooms, drained	½ teaspoon pepper
	1 cup water

Stir to blend. Cover and simmer 1 hour.

Spinach Filling:

Mix until well blended

½ cup salad oil	½ cup minced parsley
2 packages frozen chopped spinach, barely cooked	½ cup grated Parmesan cheese
2 cups bread crumbs	1½ teaspoons salt

Cook according to package directions until almost tender

1 pound seashell macaroni

Grease a 9 x 13-inch pan. Place half the cooked macaroni on bottom, top with half the spinach mixture, then half the beef mixture. Repeat the layers. Freeze. To serve, defrost and bake at 350° for 50 minutes.

ONION FRENCH BREAD
(8 to 12 servings)

Combine

½ pound softened butter	2 packages of dry onion-soup mix (1 box)

Cut in half lengthwise

2 1-pound loaves heat-and-serve French bread (use heat and serve sourdough bread if available)

Spread each of cut sides of loaves with mixture. Freeze loaves wrapped in heavy-duty aluminum foil. To serve, defrost and bake in foil at 350° for 30 minutes. Raise heat to 400° and open top of foil. Bake bread about 10 minutes longer to brown.

After the Game

HORS D'OEUVRES	Liptauer Cheese (p. 150)
	Franks in Sour Cream (p. 144)
MAIN COURSE	*Paella
	Parmesan Rolls (p. 186)
	Green Salad
DESSERT	Southern Nut Torte (p. 208)
	Coffee

PAELLA
(14 to 16 servings)

Cook until tender (about 45 minutes to 1 hour) in a large pan, in water to cover

1 3- to 4-pound chicken, cut up	Garlic
1 onion	Salt
Oregano	

Remove meat from skin and bones in large pieces. Combine

2 teaspoons oregano	1 tablespoon salt
4 peppercorns	4 tablespoons olive oil
2 cloves garlic	2 teaspoons vinegar

Brown chicken pieces in this. Add

4 ounces ham, cut in strips	2 onions, peeled and chopped
2 sliced chorizo (delicious hot Spanish sausage)	2 green peppers, chopped
	1 teaspoon coriander
	2 teaspoons capers

Cook 10 minutes over low heat. Add

6 tablespoons tomato sauce	2 cups raw rice

Cook 5 minutes. Add

4 cups boiling water	2 pounds shelled and deveined shrimp
2 teaspoons saffron shreds	

Mix well and cook in covered pan until liquid is absorbed, about 20 minutes. Mix well again. Add

Meat from 3 pounds of cooked lobster	2 10-ounce packages frozen peas

Steam open in a little water

2 quarts mussels

2 dozen small clams (use 4 dozen clams if mussels are unavailable)

Strain broth through cheesecloth over chicken, shrimp, rice mixture. Decorate with

2 cans sliced pimento

Clams, mussels

Cool quickly and freeze. Also freeze some of the shells separately and use them to decorate around the edges of the dish. Defrost to serve, reheating at 350° for 45 to 60 minutes.

Additional Suggestions for Dinner Parties:

(See the sections on cocktail parties and teas.)

Hors d'oeuvres

Cheese Boereg (p. 64)
Chicken in Crêpes (p. 89)
Cream Puffs filled with Cream Cheese and Ham (p. 98)
Cream Puffs filled with Cream Cheese and Roquefort (p. 98)
Pastry Snails (p. 100)
Shelby's Cheese Sticks (p. 104)
Tempura (p. 69)

Main Dishes

Arroz con Pollo (p. 216)
Boeuf Bourguignon (p. 226)
Cassoulet (p. 44)
Chicken Divan (p. 88)
Chicken Elizabeth (p. 180)
Chicken in Crêpes (p. 89)
Chicken Livers Risotto (p. 102)
Chicken Tetrazzini (p. 87)
Coquille Saint-Jacques (p. 185)
Duck with Fruit Stuffing (p 230)
Ham Stroganoff (p. 45)
Lasagna (p. 94)
Veal Parmesan (p. 95)

Vegetables (See the section on cooking frozen vegetables.)

Asparagus Casserole (p. 230)
Barley Pilaf (p. 227)
Green Noodles (p. 221)
Mushroom Pilaf (p. 180)
Sweet Potato Surprise (p. 231)

Salads

Cheese Fruit Freeze (p. 213)
Frozen Waldorf Salad (p. 182)
Green Pea Salad (p. 56)
Strawberry Cottage Cheese Mold (p. 217)

Breads

Brioches (p. 110)
Croissants (p. 114)
Orange Rolls (p. 224)
Parmesan Rolls (p. 186)
Crunch Sticks (p. 102)

Desserts (See the section on freezer desserts.)

Apple Pie (p. 125)
Apricot Refrigerator Cake (p. 218)
Baklava (p. 66)
Blueberry Pie (p. 128)
Chocolate Coconut Crust with Ice Cream (p. 103)
Cream Puffs with Ice Cream (p. 105)
Crêpes Fourrées (p. 92)
Crêpes Suzette (p. 92)
French Apple Pie (p. 127)
Frozen Fruits Chantilly (p. 60)
Frozen Fruits and Liqueur (p. 60)
Frozen Strawberries Romanoff (p. 60)
Pineapple Crumb Torte (p. 228)

Frozen and Fancy Free

Ladies' Luncheons

Shades of Helen Hokinson—especially if the luncheon is preceded by a morning club meeting or gathering of the ladies' literary league!

But never mind, luncheons are a delightful way to entertain an old college roommate or honor a local friend, and they also give you an opportunity to be as feminine in choice of décor, table settings and menu as your female heart desires!

There is nothing as lovely to look at as a table covered with white organdy and decorated with a bowl of pink rosebuds or yellow jonquils. And there is no better opportunity to use those recipes we classify as "ladies' luncheon" or serve the foods you just adore but your husband and children abhor.

In planning your menu include only those dishes which can be prepared in advance and, for the most part, freeze well. If your luncheon follows a meeting be especially careful to choose foods that require no more noontime preparation than heating or unmolding. Remember that you have even less time on the day of a luncheon than you do before a dinner party so save your morning for last minute tidying and table setting. With the help of your freezer you can be a guest at your own luncheon as easily as any other time you entertain.

Any of these luncheons will be enhanced with the serving of an apéritif wine before you sit down. With lunch, wine does as much for the guests as does the food!

WOMAN'S SUBURBAN DEMOCRATIC OR REPUBLICAN CLUB MORNING STUDY GROUP

* Artichoke and Crab
* Grapefruit Avocado Freeze
Brioches Miniatures (p. 110)
Vanilla Soufflé (p. 209)
Rolled Cookies (p. 198)
Tea or Coffee

ARTICHOKE AND CRAB
(12 servings)

Layer in buttered shallow casserole

  36 frozen artichoke hearts, cooked

Combine and sauté

  1½ pounds mushrooms   6 tablespoons butter

Melt

  5 tablespoons butter

Remove from heat and stir in

  6 tablespoons flour

Add gradually, stirring,

  3 cups milk

Return to heat and cook slowly, until thickened and smooth. Add and blend thoroughly

  1 cup heavy cream   ¾ cup sherry
  3 tablespoons Worcestershire   Salt and pepper
     sauce

Top artichokes with

  2¼ pounds flaked crabmeat   Cream sauce
     Mushrooms

Sprinkle over top

  ¾ cup freshly grated Parmesan   Paprika
     cheese

Freeze. To serve, defrost and bake at 375° for 40 minutes. You may substitute an equal amount of shrimp for the crabmeat.

GRAPEFRUIT AVOCADO FREEZE
(12 servings)

Blend together

  16 ounces cream cheese, softened   2 cups sour cream

Add and stir well

  ½ teaspoon salt   2 avocados, diced
  1 cup sugar   2 cups seedless grapes, halved
  2 seedless grapefruits (preferably
     pink), sectioned

Freeze in decorative mold. To serve, run knife around edge of mold; dip quickly in hot water and unmold. Take out 15 minutes before serving.

OLD COLLEGE CHUM

* CHICKEN ELIZABETH
* MUSHROOM PILAF
* ENDIVE AND BEET SALAD WITH
FRENCH DRESSING
ORANGE SHERBET WITH COINTREAU
COFFEE OR TEA

CHICKEN ELIZABETH
(12 servings)

Season

8 chicken breasts, halved

with

Salt and pepper

Brown on both sides in

¼ pound butter

Arrange in shallow baking dish. Pour over chicken a mixture of

2 pints sour cream   4 cloves garlic, pressed
1 pound crumbled Roquefort or
bleu cheese

Freeze. To serve, defrost and bake at 350° for 45 minutes.

MUSHROOM PILAF
(12 servings)

In 4-quart casserole melt

1 cup butter

Stir in and coat well

3 cups uncooked rice

Add

2 10½-ounce cans condensed onion soup	2 10½-ounce cans condensed beef consommé
	1 pound mushrooms, sliced

Bake at 325° for 45 minutes, covered. Stir occasionally. Cool quickly and freeze. When ready to serve, defrost and bake at 300° for 25 minutes. Add more consommé if mixture becomes dry.

SALAD AND DRESSING

Unfortunately there is no way to freeze the salad ingredients but both the endive and beets can be arranged in the salad bowl early in the morning, the French dressing prepared a day ahead. Either add the dressing just before serving or pass separately.

STATE-SENATOR-ELECT

* Oysters in Cream in
* Patty Shells
Orange Date Nut Bread (p. 196)
* Frozen Waldorf Salad
Pink-and-White Ice Cream Cake
Coffee or Tea

OYSTERS IN CREAM
(12 servings)

Bake frozen puff pastry patty shells in advance, according to package directions. Drain liquid into a saucepan from

4 dozen shucked oysters

Pick over oysters. Add to liquid and warm. In another saucepan, melt

½ cup butter

Remove from heat and stir in

½ cup flour

Combine

1 cup dry white wine   ½ teaspoon nutmeg
2 teaspoons salt

Add to flour mixture, stirring. Stir in

2 cups light cream

Stir constantly over fire, until thickened. Add oysters and blend. Add enough cream to bring to thin cream-sauce consistency. Stir a little of sauce into

4 beaten eggs

Then stir this into rest of cream sauce. Cool quickly and freeze. When ready to serve, defrost and warm slowly, stirring occasionally or reheat over hot water. Reheat patty shells and fill with oyster mixture.

FROZEN WALDORF SALAD
(12 servings)

In top of double boiler combine

2 eggs, slightly beaten   ½ cup pineapple juice
½ cup sugar   ¼ cup lemon juice
⅛ teaspoon salt

Cook, stirring, until thick. Cool and add

½ cup finely chopped celery   ½ cup broken nutmeats
½ cup crushed pineapple,   2 unpeeled apples finely chopped
   well drained

Fold in

1 cup heavy cream, whipped

Freeze in one large or 12 individual molds. Serve frozen on lettuce. Garnish, if desired, with mayonnaise.

NEW GIRL IN TOWN

* FRENCH ONION SOUP
* QUICHE LORRAINE
GREEN SALAD WITH FRENCH DRESSING
LEMON CRUNCH (p. 202)
TEA OR COFFEE

FRENCH ONION SOUP
(9 servings)

Peel and cut into thin slices

8 medium (approximately 1½ pounds) onions

Heat in 3 quart saucepan over low heat

5 tablespoons butter

Add onions. Cook slowly, stirring, until gold in color, about 10 minutes. Blend in gradually

2¼ quarts beef bouillon

Season with

¾ teaspoon salt   ¼ teaspoon pepper

Bring to boil. Cover saucepan and simmer about 15 minutes. Cool quickly and freeze. To serve, place under broiler, 3 inches away from heat

9 slices French bread

Toast on one side. Spread each untoasted side with some of

1 to 2 tablespoons butter

Grate

⅓ cup Swiss cheese

Sprinkle on each slice and broil again about 3 inches from heat. Meanwhile, reheat the soup. Pour the soup into a tureen or individual bowls and float toast slices on top. Serve with additional

Grated Swiss cheese

QUICHE LORRAINE
(8 servings)

Tarte Pastry:

Sift into large bowl

2 cups flour, sifted   1 teaspoon salt

Cut in

1½ sticks soft sweet butter

Work with fingers until it resembles cornmeal. Work to firm dough quickly with

⅓ cup ice water

Knead slightly. Turn out on lightly floured board and roll into a ¼-inch thick circle. Line 10-inch pie plate. Prick bottom with fork. Line with piece of buttered waxed paper and weight with rice. Bake at 375° for 30 minutes. Remove flan ring, paper and rice and bake 10 more minutes. Freeze. To serve, defrost and proceed as follows:

Cook until crisp

1 pound bacon, cut in thin pieces

Sprinkle the bottom of the pastry shell with

2 tablespoons bread crumbs   2 tablespoons grated Parmesan
Half the bacon   cheese

Fill shell with warm custard and bake at 350° for 25 minutes. Top with remaining bacon.

Custard:

Mix together

2 whole eggs   Cayenne pepper
2 egg yolks   ¼ cup bacon fat
1 teaspoon dry mustard   ¼ cup freshly grated Parmesan
1 teaspoon Dijon mustard   cheese
½ teaspoon salt

Add

2¼ cups light cream or milk, warmed

BLUSHING BRIDE

* COQUILLE SAINT-JACQUES
* PARMESAN ROLLS
FROZEN ASPARAGUS
BLACK BOTTOM CUP CAKES (p. 195)

COQUILLE SAINT-JACQUES

Simmer for 5 minutes

1 cup dry white wine or ¾ cup dry white vermouth	Pinch pepper ½ bay leaf
½ teaspoon salt	2 tablespoons minced shallots

Add

1 pound scallops	½ pound sliced mushrooms

Add enough water to barely cover ingredients. Bring to simmer. Cover and simmer for 5 minutes. Remove scallops and mushrooms and set aside. Rapidly boil down the liquid to 1 cup reduced stock. Melt

3 tablespoons butter

Remove from heat and stir in

4 tablespoons flour

Blend in

1 cup boiling reduced stock	¾ cup milk

Return to heat and boil 1 minute, take from heat. Blend together

2 egg yolks	½ cup heavy cream

Pour ¼ cup hot sauce into it—then back into remaining sauce. Return to very low heat to thicken, stirring for 2 minutes. Thin with more cream if necessary. Season with

Salt and pepper	Drops lemon juice to taste

Cut scallops crosswise into pieces. Blend two-thirds of sauce with scallops and mushrooms. Butter 6 shells or ramekins. Spoon in mixture and cover with rest of sauce. Freeze. To serve, defrost. Sprinkle with

6 tablespoons grated Swiss cheese

Dot with

1½ tablespoons butter, cut in 6 pieces

Set 8 inches from broiler and broil until browned—about 15 minutes.

PARMESAN ROLLS
(12 rolls)

Cut diagonal slits ¾ of an inch deep in

1 package dinner rolls

Mix

1 cup grated Parmesan cheese
⅓ cup mayonnaise

2 tablespoons chopped scallion
tops

Spread mixture in slits. Freeze. To serve, defrost and bake at 325° for 10 minutes, until cheese is melted.

Additional Suggestions for Luncheons:

Soups

Cheddar Cheese Soup (p. 45)
Crab Bisque (p. 220)
Gazpacho à la Sanjuan (p. 157)
Cream of Mushroom (p. 154)
Vichyssoise (p. 229)

Main Dishes

Chicken in Crêpes (p. 89)
Crêpes Filled with Crabmeat (p. 91)
Shrimp on a Green Bed (p. 169)
Chicken Divan (p. 88)
Crab and Mushroom Casserole (p. 98)
Shrimp 'n' Oysters (p. 101)

Vegetables and Salads

Cheese Fruit Freeze (p. 213)
Red-and-White Mold (p. 171)
Green Beans Chili (p. 55)
Baked Asparagus (p. 53)

Peas Suprême (p. 57)
Asparagus Casserole (p. 230)
Spinach Balls (p. 58)

Breads

Prune Bread (p. 197)
Applesauce Bread Marlowe (p. 109)
Honeybuns (p. 214)
Brioches (p. 110)
Garlic Shoestrings (p. 171)
Croissants (p. 114)
Orange Date Nut Loaf (p. 196)

Dessert

Pecan Tartes (p. 197)
Miniature Fruit Tortes (p. 130)
Southern Nut Torte (p. 208)
Cream Puffs with Ice Cream or Whipped Cream (p. 105)
Ice Cream and Sherbet with various sauces (p. 201)
Pineapple Crumb Torte (p. 228)
Apricot Refrigerator Cake (p. 218)
Sundae Pie (p. 208)
Orange Angel (p. 203)
Parisian Parfait (p. 204)
Mousse à la Maison Blanche (p. 160)
Apricot Crescents (p. 193)
Pink-and-White Cake (p. 204)

Tea for Two or Twenty-two

Teatime and springtime were made for each other. The flowers are blooming, the trees are budding and June brides "are bustin' out all over." This is such a gay and happy time of the year that

bridal entertainment is a sheer delight—for all but the poor groom and father of the bride.

At any time of year a tea is a lovely way to entertain the fair sex, whether it is for a bride-to-be or a visitor you wish your friends to meet. Unless you specifically want to have an Alice in Wonderland Tea Party, with you in the rôle of the Mad Hatter, plan and prepare in advance! Here your freezer can store absolutely everything but the tea and coffee.

Tea food should be finger food. Depending on the "elaborateness" of the board, there should be both sandwiches and pastries and possibly miniature ices. You might even include a hot canapé. For taste and appearance use a variety of breads, white and dark, and cut the sandwiches into several shapes. Ribbon, roll-up, pinwheel and open-face sandwiches are admirably suited to assembly-line production. Much of the work is time-consuming but it lends itself beautifully to companion cooking. Since these little sandwiches freeze so beautifully, you can allow yourself a great deal of time for preparation. The pastries freeze equally well and you will find that many of your favorite dessert recipes can be adapted to miniature-sized portions.

As at a buffet or cocktail party your tea table will make the first impression. The food should appeal to the eye as well as the palate. (Please, no cream cheese dyed blue!) Keep additional trays ready to replace those on the tables as they become rather raggedy about halfway through the tea. Be sure the hot beverages are hot, the cold beverages iced and the sherry at room temperature. Add clove-studded lemon slices, sugar and cream and your table is complete.

If you will play by our rules, "T" day can be spent defrosting foods, arranging trays and flowers, table setting and cat napping.

Sandwiches

General Rules:

One loaf of sandwich bread makes about 24 tea sandwiches.
Day-old bread is best unless sandwiches are to be rolled.
To remove crusts quickly use scissors.
It is easier to cut well-chilled bread.
One pound of butter spreads three medium-sized loaves.
Cream butter for ease in spreading.
Spread every slice of bread with butter to prevent filling from making bread soggy.

Freeze open-face sandwiches on trays quickly. Then pack in rigid containers or freezer bags. Other sandwiches should be wrapped first.

To defrost open-face sandwiches, spread on serving trays and cover with cloth. Defrost other sandwiches in original wrappings, opened so that moisture does not make bread soggy. Allow half an hour to an hour for defrosting at room temperature.

Sandwiches may be kept frozen up to six weeks.

Varieties:

1. OPEN-FACE made with cookie cutters. (*See illustration, p. 190.*)

2. PINWHEEL: Trim crusts from unsliced loaf. Then cut into 6 or 7 horizontal slices. Spread each slice with butter, then filling. Roll.

3. CHECKERBOARD: Make a 4-layer sandwich of trimmed slices alternating white and dark bread. Spread each slice with butter and a different spread, except top and bottom outside slices. Cut into ribbons ½ inch wide. Wrap and chill for several hours. Spread one side of each ribbon with butter. Reverse ribbons to form checkerboard loaf. To serve cut into ½-inch to ¾-inch slices while still frozen.

4. ROLLED: Trim single slices. Flatten. Butter and spread with filling. Roll up.

5. RIBBON AND FROSTED LOAF: Trim crusts from 2 unsliced loaves, 1 white, 1 dark. Cut 7 horizontal slices from each. Flatten slightly with rolling pin. Spread each with butter and a different filling, alternating dark and white slices. Top with slice of unspread bread. Makes two loaves.

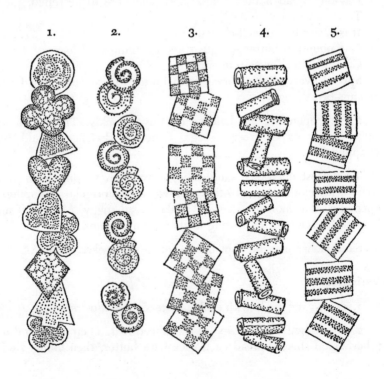

1.   2.   3.   4.   5.

FOR RIBBON: Cut into ½-inch slices before defrosting.

FOR FROSTED: Frost loaves with following mixture after defrosting. Cut several slices from loaf and serve with whole loaf on tray.

FROSTING:

Combine

16 ounces cream cheese, softened
4 tablespoons orange or pineapple juice
Few drops red or yellow food coloring (depending on juice used)

GARNISHES: Garnishes should be added before serving. Pimientos, nutmeats, parsley, rose radishes, gherkins, watercress, olives, sieved hard-cooked eggs.

Fillings:

CRABMEAT

Stir together

1½ cups crabmeat, drained and
    flaked
¼ cup mayonnaise
2 tablespoons catsup
1 tablespoon lemon juice

½ teaspoon Worcestershire sauce
¼ teaspoon salt
¼ teaspoon monosodium
    glutamate
⅛ teaspoon pepper

ALMOND OLIVE

Stir together

¾ cup toasted almonds, finely
    chopped
½ cup stuffed olives, chopped

2 tablespoons mayonnaise
1 teaspoon prepared mustard

AVOCADO

Stir together

1 cup sieved avocado
¼ cup crumbled Roquefort cheese

1 teaspoon lemon juice
¼ teaspoon garlic salt

HAM HORSERADISH

Stir together

2 cups ground cooked ham
¼ cup minced parsley

2 tablespoons thick sour cream
2 tablespoons horseradish

CHICKEN BACON

Stir together

8 slices crisp bacon, crumbled
1 cup finely chopped cooked
   chicken
¼ cup mayonnaise
1 tablespoon finely chopped
   pimiento

¼ teaspoon salt
¼ teaspoon monosodium
   glutamate
⅛ teaspoon pepper

TOASTED PECAN

Stir together

3-ounce package softened
   cream cheese
1 cup toasted pecans,
   finely chopped

¾ cup crushed pineapple,
   well drained

COGNAC CHEESE

Beat together

3-ounce package softened
   cream cheese
⅓ cup crumbled Roquefort cheese
3 tablespoons sour cream

1½ teaspoons Worcestershire
   sauce
2 drops tabasco
1 tablespoon cognac

ORANGE CHEESE

Beat together

3-ounce package softened
   cream cheese
2 tablespoons orange marmalade

¼ teaspoon salt
⅞ teaspoon paprika

BUTTER SPREADS

Beat until soft and creamy

½ cup butter

Add one or more slowly

1 teaspoon lemon juice
1 teaspoon Worcestershire sauce
1 teaspoon dry mustard

1 teaspoon grated onion or
minced garlic

To make various spreads add:

4 tablespoons chopped chives
½ cup grated or soft cheese
2 tablespoons anchovy paste,
or to taste

4 tablespoons horseradish
4 tablespoons catsup or chili sauce
2 tablespoons chutney

For Hot Canapés see:

Cheese Savories (p. 142)
Cheese Lobster Rolls (p. 141)
Cream Puffs filled with Cream Cheese and Ham (p. 98)
Cream Puffs filled with Cream Cheese and Roquefort (p. 98)
Pastry Snails (p. 100)
Sausage Balls in Pastry Blankets (p. 147)
Shelby's Cheese Sticks (p. 104)
Smithfield Ham in Biscuits

Additional Suggestions for Spreads:

Liptauer Cheese (p. 150)
Tipsy Cheese (p. 150)

Pastries

APRICOT CRESCENTS
(Makes 30)

Cut together

½ cup soft butter

6-ounce package softened
cream cheese

into

¾ cup sifted flour   ⅛ teaspoon salt

Add

1 tablespoon cold water

Mix with fork until well blended. Chill at least 1 hour. Roll into thin rectangle on well-floured board. Cut into 30 2½ x 3-inch rectangles. Spread each piece with

2 tablespoons apricot preserves

Sprinkle with

1 cup finely chopped nuts

Roll up from one corner and bend ends to form crescents. Put folded side down on cookie sheet and bake at 450° for 10 minutes. When cool, sprinkle with

Confectioners' sugar

Freeze. Thaw in about 15 minutes.

BANANA CAKE

Cream together

¼ pound butter   1 cup sugar

Add and beat well

2 eggs   4 tablespoons sour cream

Sift together

1 teaspoon baking powder   1½ cups cake flour, sifted
1 teaspoon baking soda   1 pinch salt

Slowly beat the dry ingredients into the liquid ingredients. Mix in

2 ripe bananas, mashed   1 teaspoon vanilla

Bake at 350° for 40 minutes in a tube pan. Cool and sprinkle with

Confectioners' sugar

Freeze. To serve, defrost.

BLACK BOTTOM CUP CAKES
(Makes 1½ dozen)

Cream Cheese Mixture:

Combine in mixing bowl and mix well

8 ounces cream cheese, softened	½ cup sugar
1 egg	⅛ teaspoon salt

Stir in

6 ounces semisweet chocolate bits

Cocoa Batter:

Sift together

1½ cups flour	¼ cup cocoa
1 cup sugar	½ teaspoon salt

Add to dry ingredients and beat well

1 cup water	1 tablespoon vinegar
⅓ cup cooking oil	1 teaspoon vanilla

Fill miniature muffin tins, which have been lined with paper muffin cups, one-third full with

Cocoa batter

Top each with

1 heaping tablespoon cream-cheese mixture

Bake at 350° for 30 to 35 minutes. Freeze. To serve, defrost.

CHINESE WALNUT COOKIES
(7 dozen)

Sift together

3 cups flour	1 teaspoon baking powder

Stir in

1½ cups sugar

Cut in with pastry blender

   1 cup butter

Stir in

   2 beaten eggs   1 teaspoon almond extract
   1 tablespoon light corn syrup   1 cup ground walnuts
   1 teaspoon vanilla

Shape into walnut-sized balls. Place 2 inches apart on ungreased cookie sheet. Beat together

   1 egg   1 tablespoon water

Brush tops of cookies with egg mixture. Press onto each top

   ½ walnut

Bake at 450° until golden, about 10 minutes. Freeze. Defrost to serve.

ORANGE DATE AND NUT LOAF

Squeeze the juice from

   1 large orange

Add

   Boiling water

to make 1 cup. Put through food chopper

   Orange rind

Add

   Enough dates

to fill 1 cup. Place orange mixture in bowl. Add orange-juice mixture. Stir in

   1 teaspoon baking soda   2 tablespoons melted shortening
   1 cup sugar   1 teaspoon vanilla

Add

   1 beaten egg   ¼ teaspoon salt
   2 cups flour   ½ cup chopped nuts
   1 teaspoon baking powder

Bake in greased loaf pan at 350° for 1 hour. Cool and freeze. Defrost and serve very thinly sliced with butter or cream cheese.

PECAN TARTES

Crust:

Sift together

1½ cups sifted flour   ½ teaspoon salt

Cut in with pastry blender

½ cup shortening

until pieces are the size of small peas. Sprinkle approximately

4 tablespoons cold water

one at a time, on mixture. Mix with fork. Repeat until dough is moistened.

It is of good consistency when it does not stick to your hands when you gather it up to form into a ball. It will handle more easily if chilled for half an hour. Roll out on floured board, turning as you roll. Cut into rounds 1¾ inches in diameter and fit into miniature muffin tins.

Pecan Filling:

Cream

⅓ cup butter   ¾ cup firmly packed brown sugar

Beat in one at a time

3 eggs

Stir in

1 cup light corn syrup   1 teaspoon vanilla
1 cup broken pecan meats   ¼ teaspoon salt

Fill each shell with filling and top with

½ pecan

Bake at 375° for 15 to 20 minutes, until filling is set. Freeze. To serve, defrost.

PRUNE BREAD

Soak in bowl of cold water for 1 hour

½ pound prunes

Drain, pit and cut up the prunes. Add

¾ cup boiling water   1 teaspoon baking soda

Let stand 5 minutes. Add

¾ cup sugar
1 egg
1¾ cups flour

½ teaspoon salt
2 tablespoons melted shortening

Bake bread in greased loaf pan at 325° for 40 minutes. Cool and freeze.
To serve, defrost; slice thinly and spread with butter or cream cheese.

ROLLED COOKIES
(4 dozen)

In mixer combine well

¾ cup sugar
3 beaten eggs
½ pound melted butter
3 heaping tablespoons sour cream

3½ cups sifted flour
2 teaspoons baking powder
Pinch baking soda
Pinch salt

*Chill about 1 hour before handling. Divide into 7 pieces. Roll each piece
out onto floured board in rectangle. Spread with*

Raisins
Chopped walnuts
Jelly (your choice)

Cinnamon
Sugar

Roll up each section like a jelly roll and arrange on greased cookie sheets.
Bake at 350° for 30 minutes. Cool and freeze. Defrost and slice very thin
to serve.

SCHNECKEN

Mix with fingers until well blended

3 cups flour

½ pound butter

Mix together

3 egg yolks
1 cup heavy cream

¼ cup milk

Add to first mixture and blend well. Sprinkle over top of dough

1 package dry yeast

Mix in. Divide into 6 parts and wrap each in foil. Refrigerate overnight.
Roll each package into a circle on floured board. Combine

1 cup chopped walnuts or pecans   2½ teaspoon cinnamon
1½ cups sugar

Divide this mixture into 6 portions and place each circle *on top* of one
of these portions. Press down. Then turn it over and repeat so both sides
are covered by mixture. Cut each circle in 8 wedges like a pie. Roll up
each wedge starting at wide end. Bake on greased cookie sheet at 325°
for 25 minutes. Freeze. To serve, defrost.

Additional Suggestions for Pastries:

Apricot Fruitcake, cut in small, thin slices (p. 109)
Butterscotch Bars (p. 111)
Cinnamon Horns (p. 114)
Florentines (p. 117)
Miniature Fruit Tortes (p. 130)
Miniature Cream Puffs (p. 98)
Orange Balls (p. 119)
Oatmeal Toll House Cookies (p. 118)
Pound Cake (p. 99)
Toffee Squares (p. 121)
Applesauce Bread cut in small, thin slices (p. 109)

THE END OF A PERFECT DAY

Freezer Desserts

Once upon a time—not long ago, merely a cookbook or two
away—a chapter on freezer desserts contained recipes ranging from
vanilla ice cream to chocolate. This may be a slight exaggeration
since you could make sherbets and ices too! Today, homemade
ice cream is only for the purist since commercial firms have
taken over the task and have been quite successful from the stand-
point of taste and quality. The housewife has been "emancipated"

from the ice-cream machine but only in order to create frozen culinary masterpieces, utilizing ready-made ice creams!

To end the perfect day and the perfect meal, a beautiful dessert is always welcome. Desserts that come from the freezer seem to be lighter and more refreshing and therefore are particularly appropriate after a heavy meal or on hot summer evenings. They have the further advantage of requiring no last-minute work other than slight defrosting to soften them.

Actually the majority of dessert recipes can be frozen if you wish, but in this chapter we will treat only those recipes that must be frozen until just before serving time. We have included several ice-cream variations and desserts made with ice cream as well as a few others that require freezing. In the chapters on holiday baking, weekend guests, etc., you will find other desserts which can be classified as "optional freezables."

Ice Cream and Sherbet Variations

Coffee Ice Cream with: Crème de Cacao, Crème de Menthe (white), Kahlua, Dark Rum

Maple Walnut Ice Cream with: Anisette

Pistachio Ice Cream with: Claret Sauce

Peach Ice Cream with: Cherry Heering, Cointreau

Vanilla Ice Cream with: Guava Jelly and juice of 1 lime and ¼ cup rum; melted plum jelly, or just about anything!

Lemon Sherbet with: Cointreau, Crème de Menthe (green), Curaçao, Rum

Orange Sherbet with: Cointreau, Grand Marnier

Pineapple Sherbet with: Crème de Menthe (green)

Raspberry Sherbet with: Triple Sec

Garnishes:

Almonds, toasted and chopped
Coconut, grated, shredded, toasted
Chocolate, shaved bittersweet
Macaroons, crumbled
Peanut brittle, crushed
Peppermint stick candy, crushed
Whipped Cream

Every variety of frozen fruit, barely thawed and flavored with brandy, rum or other suitable liqueur.

ICE CREAM PIE SPECTACULAR
(8 servings)

Generously butter a 9-inch pie plate

Beat until frothy

1 egg white   ¼ teaspoon salt

Gradually add, beating well after each addition

¼ cup sugar

Continue beating until stiff. Fold in

    1½ cups chopped walnuts

Place in pie plate. Spread evenly with spoon over bottom and sides, building up sides. Prick with fork. Bake at 400° for 10 to 12 minutes until lightly brown. Cool, then chill. Spoon evenly into shell

    1 pint coffee ice cream

Top with

    1 pint vanilla ice cream

Freeze until serving time. Then top with Raisin Caramel Sauce.

Raisin Caramel Sauce:

In small saucepan heat

    3 tablespoons butter

Add and heat slowly, stirring constantly until smooth, about 10 minutes

    1 cup firmly packed brown sugar

Remove from heat and add slowly, stirring

    ½ cup medium or heavy cream

Heat one minute more. Stir in

    ½ cup golden raisins   1 teaspoon vanilla

Refrigerate if desired. Reheat to serve.

LEMON CRUNCH
(8 servings)

Crust:

Combine

    1½ cups graham-cracker crumbs   ½ cup melted butter

Press half into 8 x 8-inch pan or 9-inch pie plate.

Filling:

Cook until clear

    1 tablespoon cornstarch   ¾ cup boiling water
    ⅔ cup sugar

Add

⅛ teaspoon salt   2 egg yolks
2 teaspoons grated lemon rind

Cook over boiling water, stirring, until egg thickens. Remove from heat.

Add

4 tablespoons lemon juice

Chill. Beat until stiff

2 egg whites

Fold into lemon mixture. Fold in

1¼ cups heavy cream, whipped

Pour into crumb-lined pan. Top with remaining crumbs. Freeze until serving time.

You may substitute oranges or limes using same quantities of rind and juice.

ORANGE ANGEL
(8 servings)

Split horizontally into 3 layers

1 large angel cake

Place top layer with cut side down, on plate. Spoon over layer

1 pint orange sherbet

Top with second cake layer. Spoon over

1 pint orange sherbet

Top with last layer, crust side up. Whip until stiff

2 cups heavy cream

Tint a pale yellow with

Yellow food coloring

Frost entire cake. Sprinkle top and sides with

1 cup finely grated lemon peel

Freeze. To serve, defrost in refrigerator for 1½ hours.

PARISIAN PARFAIT
(6 to 8 servings)

Combine in saucepan

4 tablespoons cocoa
⅓ cup hot water
½ tablespoon butter

¼ cup honey
¼ cup white corn syrup
¼ teaspoon vanilla

Cook until boiling. Remove from heat and stir in

⅛ cup bourbon

Place in parfait glasses alternate layers of

1 quart vanilla ice cream   Chocolate-bourbon sauce

Keep in freezer until serving time. Top with

Whipped cream

PINK-AND-WHITE CAKE
(12 to 14 servings)

Split into 3 layers

9-inch sponge or orange-chiffon cake

Place in round loaf pan. Sprinkle first layer with

⅛ cup sweet sherry

Cover with half of

¾ cup currant jelly

Place on top

1 pint vanilla ice cream

then

1 pint raspberry sherbet

Put on second layer of cake. Sprinkle with

⅛ cup sweet sherry   1 pint vanilla ice cream
Remainder of currant jelly

Top with third cake layer. Freeze at least two hours. Unmold on plate. Cover top and sides with

1 cup heavy cream, whipped

Dust with

2 tablespoons ground pistachio nuts

Freeze. To serve, place in refrigerator for 30 minutes.

SNOWBALLS WITH CHOCOLATE SAUCE

Scoop balls of

Any flavor ice cream

Roll in

Grated coconut

Freeze. Serve topped with following chocolate sauce

or

Roll in mixture of

1½ teaspoons instant coffee powder   1⅓ cups grated coconut
1½ teaspoons water

Chocolate Sauce:

Melt in top of double boiler

6 squares unsweetened chocolate   ⅔ cup water

Add

1⅓ cups sugar

Boil gently over direct heat for 4 minutes, stirring constantly. Remove from heat, cool and beat in

¼ cup butter

Freeze. To serve, defrost and reheat carefully.

Hot Soufflés! Frozen Only

Believe it or not there is a way to serve hot soufflés without making them at the last minute. It is absolutely necessary to freeze the soufflés immediately after making so that the egg whites cannot collapse. Of course you may also bake and serve immediately.

RASPBERRY GRAPE SOUFFLÉS
(12 servings)

Halve

  1½ cups seedless grapes

Blend the grapes with

  ¾ cup raspberry jam

Spread the mixture in the bottom of 12 buttered individual ovenproof casseroles. In saucepan combine

  9 tablespoons sugar   1½ inches vanilla-bean seeds
  9 tablespoons flour   ¼ teaspoon salt

Gradually add and stir until smooth

  2¼ cups milk

Cook over moderate heat, stirring, until thick and smooth. Remove from heat, cool slightly, add

  9 egg yolks, lightly beaten

Beat until stiff

  9 egg whites

Fold egg whites into soufflé mixture. Pour over the raspberry mixture in individual ovenproof soufflé dishes. Freeze immediately. When frozen, remove the soufflés from the soufflé dishes. It will be necessary to run a knife around the edge of the dish. Place the soufflés in a flat pan and cover well with freezer paper. Return to freezer. To serve, return to buttered soufflé dishes and place in 400° oven. Immediately reduce the temperature to 375° and bake for 20 to 30 minutes until puffed and no longer runny in the center.

Sprinkle with

Confectioners' sugar

Serve immediately.

ORANGE SOUFFLÉS
(12 servings)

Rub

6 large lumps sugar

over

Rind of two oranges

Crush the sugar lumps, grate the orange peel and add to

9 tablespoons sugar	1 inch vanilla-bean seeds
9 tablespoons flour	¼ teaspoon salt

Gradually add and stir until smooth

2¼ cups milk

Cook over moderate heat, stirring, until thick and smooth. Remove from heat. Add

9 egg yolks, lightly beaten	½ cup orange liqueur (Cointreau, Curaçao, Grand Marnier, etc.)

Beat until stiff

9 egg whites

Fold egg whites into soufflé mixture. Pour the mixture into 12 buttered individual ovenproof soufflé dishes. Freeze immediately. When frozen, remove the soufflés from the soufflé dishes. It will be necessary to run a knife around the edge of the dish. Place the soufflés in a flat pan and cover well with freezer paper. Return to freezer. To serve, return to buttered soufflé dishes and place in 400° oven. Immediately reduce the temperature to 375° and bake for 20 to 30 minutes until puffed and no longer runny in the center.

Sprinkle with

Confectioners' sugar

Serve immediately.

SOUTHERN NUT TORTE
(8 servings)

Beat until light and fluffy

2 eggs   1 teaspoon vanilla

Fold in

1 cup sugar   1 cup chopped pecans
1 cup crushed Ritz cracker
  crumbs

Spread mixture in greased 9-inch pie plate. Build up edges. Bake at 350° for 10 to 15 minutes until crisp and dry. Cool. Top with

1 pint softened vanilla ice cream

Freeze. Before serving thaw for 15 minutes at room temperature.

SUNDAE PIE
(8 servings)

Crust:

In 9-inch pie plate make and bake cookie pie crust as directed on icebox cookie dough roll, using

¾ roll of butterscotch nut icebox cookie dough

Chill well.

Sauce:

Over hot, not boiling water melt

¾ cup semisweet chocolate bits   3 tablespoons water
3 tablespoons white corn syrup

Beat until smooth. Refrigerate.

Meringue:

In small bowl beat until soft peaks form

3 egg whites   Pinch of salt

Gradually add

6 tablespoons sugar

Beat until stiff.

Fill shell with

1 quart softened vanilla ice cream

Pour over ice cream

2 tablespoons sauce

Cover with meringue

Be sure meringue touches edge of pie all around. Drizzle on rest of sauce. Marbleize with knife. Bake at 500° for 2 minutes. Freeze. Before serving put in refrigerator for 1 hour.

TORTONI
(6 servings)

Grind in electric blender enough

Hard macaroons

to make ½ cup plus 2 tablespoons. Beat

1 cup heavy cream

Fold in

½ cup macaroon crumbs	1 egg white, stiffly beaten
⅓ cup sifted confectioners' sugar	1 tablespoon sherry

Pour mixture into

2-inch paper baking cups

Sprinkle with remaining 2 tablespoons crumbs. Freeze. To serve, defrost for 5 minutes.

VANILLA SOUFFLÉ
(6 servings)

Soften slightly

1 pint vanilla ice cream

Stir in

6 crumbled macaroons   4 teaspoons Grand Marnier

Fold in

½ cup heavy cream, whipped

Spoon into 3-cup mold. Sprinkle with

2 tablespoons chopped toasted almonds   1 to 2 teaspoons confectioners' sugar

Freeze. Serve with following sauce.

Sauce:

Simmer until soft, not mushy

10-ounce package frozen strawberries   Sugar to taste

Stir in

4 teaspoons Grand Marnier

Refrigerate until serving.

Additional Suggestions for Freezer Desserts:

Holiday Ice Cream Cake (p. 118)
Cream Puffs filled with Ice Cream (p. 105)
Cherry Sundae (p. 59)
Chocolate Coconut Crust with Ice Cream (p. 103)
Peachy-Orange Sauce and Ice Cream (p. 61)
Puff Pastry Shells filled with Ice Cream (p. 105)

FRIDAY TO MONDAY

Feeding Weekend Guests

In this chapter on the entertaining of weekend guests we have come full circle from that day when the spanking new freezer arrived at your home and you began to fill it. Much of what we have

written in the preceding chapters comes into play when you have houseguests.

Gracious weekend entertaining is not a lost art nor is it confined to landed gentry in the English countryside. It is, however, the most demanding type of hostessing and requires a great deal of skill and tact to keep your household running smoothly and your guests comfortable. Both of your authors, one a suburbanite and the other a resident of the nation's capital, are addicted to such entertaining and find it a delightful pastime, worthy of some care and planning.

If we have seemed to place great emphasis on planning as the most important prerequisite to any well-run household, in this chapter we cannot possibly emphasize it enough. *Leave nothing undone that can be done before your guests arrive.* Needless to say, this includes cleaning and shopping, but in addition all of your cooking (with the exception of the coffee and breakfast eggs) should be completed too! More than likely your menus will be somewhat more elaborate than the usual family fare and you will probably have to plan about six meals: Friday dinner, Saturday breakfast, lunch and dinner, Sunday breakfast and dinner. The number will vary depending on when your guests arrive and depart, if any meals will be eaten away from home and whether you can get away with brunch in place of breakfast and lunch.

You may also want to have some friends in to meet your guests and for such entertaining we refer you to the sections on party foods. If you rely on frozen dishes for all your meals and party foods you will be relaxed enough and have enough time to enjoy your company, which is, after all, why you invited them.

There are few houseguests who will not pitch in for table setting, dishwashing and bedmaking in the servantless household. (The few slackers who have darkened our doorstep have never been invited back!) With their help and the help of your freezer you may find yourself with a great deal more free time than you ever expected!

Think of our friend with whose problems we began the first chapter. The mother of six, she was expecting weekend guests with *their* six children. She followed our suggestions, filled her freezer and thoroughly enjoyed her company. You can do it too if you will freeze with ease and relax!

FRIDAY DINNER

FRANKS 'N' KRAUT (p. 143)
* SEAFOOD CASSEROLE
* CHEESE FRUIT FREEZE
PARTY SQUASH (p. 56)
* HONEYBUNS
* TOFFEE CRUNCH CAKE
BEVERAGE

SEAFOOD CASSEROLE
(12 servings)

Barely cook and drain

1 pound shell macaroni

Heat together

2 cans frozen cream of lobster
   soup

2 6-ounce cans sliced mushrooms

2 tablespoons lemon juice

2 cups shredded cheese

2 teaspoons soy sauce

2 teaspoons celery salt

Add

2 pounds crabmeat

3 cups cooked shrimp

Put macaroni in bottom of buttered casserole. Pour hot mixture over it. Cool quickly and freeze. To serve, defrost and bake at 375° for 30 minutes.

CHEESE FRUIT FREEZE
(10 to 12 servings)

Drain and dice, reserving 2 tablespoons syrup

1 1-pound 13-ounce can cling peaches

Drain

1 1-pound can grapefruit sections

Drain

2 cans pitted Bing cherries

Sprinkle

1 package gelatin (1 tablespoon)

over

2 tablespoons peach syrup

Let stand 5 minutes, dissolve over hot water. Soften

1 6-ounce package cream cheese

and whip with

    ¼ cup milk

Whip

    ½ cup heavy cream

Fold into cheese mixture with

⅓ cup mayonnaise	¼ teaspoon dry mustard
½ teaspoon salt	2 tablespoons lemon juice

Add a little cheese mixture to gelatin, then stir gelatin into rest of cheese mixture. Fold in fruits. Pour into rinsed fancy mold. Freeze until firm. When ready to serve, loosen around edges with knife; dip quickly into hot water and unmold on serving plate about 15 minutes before serving.

HONEYBUNS
(18 rolls)

Place close to each other in two 8-inch pans

    18 cloverleaf brown-and-serve rolls

Combine

¾ cup honey	6 tablespoons brown sugar
¾ teaspoon cinnamon	¾ cup broken pecans

Spoon this over the rolls. Freeze. To serve, defrost and bake at 400° for 15 to 20 minutes.

TOFFEE CRUNCH CAKE
(12 servings)

In large bowl mix like a pie crust

1 cup white sugar	1 teaspoon baking soda
1 cup brown sugar	½ teaspoon salt
½ cup butter	½ teaspoon vanilla
2 cups flour, sifted	

Take out ½ cup and reserve for topping. To the remaining add

1 cup buttermilk	1 egg

Beat thoroughly. Pour into greased 9 x 13-inch pan

Combine

Reserved mixture

6 Heath candy bars, chopped   **½ cup chopped pecans**

Sprinkle over batter. Bake at 350° for 30 to 35 minutes. Cool and freeze.
To serve, defrost.

SATURDAY BREAKFAST

JUICE
* POPOVERS
OMELETTE
COFFEE, MILK

POPOVERS
(12 servings)

Into a bowl break

4 eggs

Add

2 cups milk   **1 teaspoon salt**
2 cups flour, sifted

Mix until eggs are blended. Disregard lumps. Pour batter into 12 well-
greased 5-ounce custard cups, three-quarters full. Set into muffin tins or
onto a cookie sheet. Place in cold oven. Set oven at 450°. Turn on heat.
Do not open oven for half an hour. Remove popovers from oven. Puncture
four sides of neck. Return to oven for 10 minutes with heat off. Freeze.
To serve, place popovers on cookie sheet without touching each other;
heat in 350° oven 7 to 10 minutes.

SATURDAY LUNCH

TOMATO JUICE
* ITALIAN RICE BAKE
GREEN SALAD
SHERBET
BEVERAGE

ITALIAN RICE BAKE
(12 to 14 servings)

Sauté until lightly browned

3 medium onions, minced
1½ pounds sweet Italian or
   fresh sausage, broken up

6 tablespoons butter

Add

6 packages frozen artichokes

1½ 15-ounce packages frozen peas

Brown lightly and add

1 9-ounce can broiled-in-butter
   chopped mushrooms

1½ cups canned beef bouillon

Simmer uncovered for 10 minutes. Stir in

9 cups cooked rice

2 cans beef bouillon

Toss lightly. Turn into greased casserole. Freeze. To serve, defrost; sprinkle top with

1½ cups shredded Parmesan cheese

Bake 45 to 60 minutes at 375°.

SATURDAY DINNER

SMITHFIELD HAM IN BISCUITS (p. 148)
WINE NUT ROLLS (p. 150)
* ARROZ CON POLLO
* STRAWBERRY COTTAGE CHEESE MOLD
CRUNCH STICKS (p. 102)
* APRICOT REFRIGERATOR CAKE
COFFEE

ARROZ CON POLLO
(12 servings)

In a large skillet, combine and sauté until golden

3 2½- to 3-pound fryers, quartered   ¾ cup olive oil

Chop fine and add

6 cloves garlic
3 medium onions, sautéed until brown

9 medium green peppers

Add

6 tomatoes, peeled, seeded and cut into small pieces

Cook 2 minutes. Place in casserole and add

¾ teaspoon red pepper
10½ cups chicken broth

15 grains saffron

Freeze. To serve, defrost and add

4½ cups rice, uncooked

Bake at 400° for 20 minutes. Remove and decorate with

1 pound slightly defrosted peas
3 4-ounce jars pimientos, cut in strips

3 packages slightly defrosted artichokes

Cover and bake in 350° oven for 25 to 30 minutes, or until rice is tender. Do not stir casserole.

STRAWBERRY COTTAGE CHEESE MOLD
(12 to 14 servings)

Partially defrost

4 10-ounce packages frozen strawberries

Discard

⅔ cup juice

Combine

2 cups sour cream

4 cups cottage cheese

Fold in

⅓ teaspoon salt

Strawberries

Pour into mold and freeze. Unmold to serve, without defrosting.

APRICOT REFRIGERATOR CAKE
(12 to 14 servings)

Stew until tender and liquid is absorbed

1 12-ounce box dried apricots	2 cups water

Press through sieve and cool. Cream

1 cup butter	2 cups confectioners' sugar

Add one at a time, beating after each addition

4 egg yolks

Beat in

Apricot puree	Grated rind and juice of 1 lemon

Beat stiff

4 egg whites

Beat into whites

⅓ cup sugar

Fold egg-white mixture into apricot mixture. Line sides and bottom of a 9-inch spring form with

3 packages split ladyfingers

Put in alternate layers of

⅓ of apricot mixture	⅓ of remaining ladyfingers

Freeze. When ready to serve defrost and remove sides of spring form. Garnish with

1 cup heavy cream, whipped	Whole canned drained apricots
⅓ cup toasted slivered almonds	Sprigs of whole mint

SUNDAY BRUNCH

STEWED FRUITS (p. 132)
* DANISH PUFF
SAUSAGE AND SCRAMBLED EGGS
COFFEE

DANISH PUFF
(Serves 14 to 16)

Measure into a bowl

1 cup sifted flour

Cut in

½ cup butter

Sprinkle over this and mix with fork

2 tablespoons water

Roll into ball and divide in half. Pat dough with hands into 2 long strips, 3 inches x 12 inches. Place strips 3 inches apart on ungreased cookie sheet.

Mix together and bring to a rolling boil

½ cup butter   1 cup water

Add

1 teaspoon almond extract

Remove from heat. Stir in immediately

1 cup sifted flour

Beat in, one at a time

3 eggs

When smooth, divide mixture in half; spread each half of mixture over each piece of pastry. Bake at 350° for 50 minutes, until topping is puffed, crisp and light brown. Frost the puff while still warm with following mixture

2 tablespoons butter   Juice and grated rind of ¾ of
1 cup confectioners' sugar   a lemon

Top with

Slivered almonds

Freeze. To serve, defrost and reheat in 350° oven.

SUNDAY DINNER

* CRAB BISQUE
* BRAISED YANKEE POT ROAST
* GREEN NOODLES
CARROTS AND PEAS, FROZEN
SMALL BOILED ONIONS
APPLESAUCE WITH CRANBERRIES (p. 127)
* BLACK-AND-WHITE ROLL
COFFEE OR TEA

CRAB BISQUE
(16 servings)

Combine and bring to a boil

4 cups beef bouillon
2 cans condensed tomato soup

2 cans condensed green-pea soup

Add:

1 pound crabmeat

1 cup light cream

Freeze. To serve, defrost and heat. Add

½ cup dry sherry

Season to taste.

BRAISED YANKEE POT ROAST
(12 servings)

Combine in a kettle

2 cups red wine
4 tablespoons vinegar
6 peppercorns

2 bay leaves
2 garlic cloves, crushed
½ teaspoon sage

Marinate overnight

6 pound top round, boneless rump, etc., roast

Remove meat from marinade. Brown in

½ cup shortening

Season with

2 tablespoons salt

Add marinade and

4 cups canned tomatoes   2 cups tomato puree

Bring to a boil. Cover and simmer 4 hours. Add

2 cups beef consommé

Cool quickly and freeze. To serve, defrost and cook about 1 hour longer, until beef is tender. Remove meat and keep warm. Boil sauce about 20 minutes to reduce it. While sauce is boiling cook

1½ pounds frozen carrots and peas   24 small white onions

Slice meat. Arrange meat on platter with vegetables and gravy.

GREEN NOODLES
(12 servings)

Cook according to package directions

2 pounds green noodles

Melt

1½ cups butter

Add to butter

3 cups freshly grated Parmesan   1 cup heavy cream
cheese

Cook over low heat until blended and smooth; stir. Drain the noodles and toss with the hot sauce. Freeze. To serve, defrost and reheat in double boiler or over low flame, stirring.

BLACK-AND-WHITE ROLL
(16 servings)

White Roll:

Beat until thick and light in color

4 eggs
¾ teaspoon baking powder

¼ teaspoon salt

Gradually add

¾ cup sugar

1 teaspoon vanilla

Fold in

¾ cup sifted cake flour

Turn into 15 x 10 x 2-inch jelly-roll pan, lined with greased paper. Bake at 400° for 13 minutes. Turn pan out onto towel, dusted with

Confectioners' sugar

Remove paper and cut off crisp edges immediately. Roll like jelly roll with towel inside and covering the outside.

Black Roll:

Beat until light

5 egg yolks

Add gradually

1 cup confectioners' sugar

Blend in well

¼ cup sifted flour
1 teaspoon salt   } sifted together
3 tablespoons cocoa

Beat in

1 teaspoon vanilla

Fold in

5 stiffly beaten egg whites

Turn into same-sized pan, lined as above. Bake at 375° for 15 to 20 minutes. After baking treat as white roll above, without confectioners' sugar. Freeze both rolls as wrapped with additional freezing wrap. Defrost at room temperature, after removing freezing wrap. Remove towel, spread one-third of following filling over top of opened white roll. Place black roll, opened, on top of white roll. Spread with half of remaining filling. Roll both rolls up together as jelly roll and cover with remaining filling. Refrigerate until serving time.

Filling:

Combine and chill for 1 hour

3 cups heavy cream	1 cup sugar
⅔ cup cocoa	

Then whip until stiff.

FRIDAY DINNER

LIPTAUER CHEESE (p. 150)
* CHICKEN PAPRIKA
* BOULGHOUR PILAF
* ORANGE ROLLS
GRAPEFRUIT AVOCADO FREEZE (p. 179)
FRUIT KUCHEN (p. 117)

CHICKEN PAPRIKA
(8 servings)

Melt in a large skillet

½ cup butter

Add and brown slowly, 10 to 15 minutes

2 2½- to 3-pound chickens, cut up

Sprinkle with

1 tablespoon paprika	Dash pepper
2 teaspoons salt	

Add

½ cup chopped onion

Cover and cook over low heat 20 minutes. Cool and freeze. To serve, defrost and reheat in skillet. Add

2 cups sour cream   2 teaspoons lemon juice

Adjust seasonings. Cook until sour cream is heated through.

BOULGHOUR PILAF
(8 to 10 servings)

Braise for 5 minutes

3 cups Boulghour   ¼ pound melted butter
(cracked wheat)

On the side fry

1 onion, chopped

Add to the Boulghour with

6 cups chicken stock

Cover and bake at 350° for 25 minutes. Freeze. To serve, defrost; bake at 350° for 15 to 20 minutes, until tender.

ORANGE ROLLS
(12 rolls)

Cream to a smooth paste

2 tablespoons soft butter   Grated rind of 1 orange
2 teaspoons orange juice   ½ cup powdered sugar

Freeze. To serve, defrost and spread thickly on

12 brown-and-serve rolls, baked

Return to 350° oven for 1 minute to make the topping runny and hot.

SATURDAY BREAKFAST

ORANGE PINEAPPLE JUICE
BRIOCHES (p. 110)
POACHED EGGS AND HAM STEAK
BEVERAGE

SATURDAY LUNCH

* PIZZA
LETTUCE AND TOMATO
ICE CREAM
BEVERAGE

PIZZA
(6 to 8 servings)

Dough:

Combine and stir until dissolved

1 package dry yeast   2 tablespoons warm water

Combine

1 cup boiling water   2 tablespoons shortening

Cool and add to yeast mixture. Add

3 cups flour   1½ teaspoons salt

Combine to make a ball; divide into two balls. Grease two pizza pans, 14 inches in diameter. With well-greased hands pat each ball of dough into pizza pan to cover bottom and lap over side.

Spread each crust with

2 tablespoons oil

Sauce:

Combine

>   2 8-ounce cans tomato sauce   2 cloves garlic, minced
>   1 6-ounce can tomato paste   Salt and pepper

Pour sauce over crusts.

Topping:

Sprinkle on top of sauce contents of

>   2 8-ounce packages provolone   2 pounds Italian sausage
>   cheese, diced   (hot and sweet mixed)
>   4 green peppers, chopped

Freeze. To serve, defrost and bake at 500° for 30 minutes, until cheese
is melted and bubbly and crust is brown.

SATURDAY DINNER

CHEESE LOBSTER ROLLS (p. 141)
MINIATURE QUICHE (p. 145)
* BOEUF BOURGUIGNON
* BARLEY PILAF
GREEN SALAD
* PINEAPPLE CRUMB TORTE
COFFEE

BOEUF BOURGUIGNON
(8 to 10 servings)

Put in cold water

>   3 pounds lean salt pork, diced

*Bring to a slow boil, cover and simmer for 10 minutes. Drain; rinse the
pork in cold water and dry. Sauté (until pork is yellow)*

>   Diced salt pork   Salt and pepper to taste
>   24 small white onions, peeled   6 tablespoons lard

Remove the onions with a slotted spoon and add

4 cups finely chopped mushrooms   Salt and pepper to taste

Remove mushrooms with a slotted spoon and sprinkle

4 pounds stew-beef cubes (chuck)

with

Salt and pepper   Thyme
Bay leaf   4 tablespoons flour

Sauté in lard left in pan until brown on all sides. Place meat in baking dish with

Bouquet garni (bay leaf, thyme, parsley tied in small piece of cheese-cloth)

Pour over meat

3 cups red Burgundy   5 cups beef stock

Cover and cook at 325° for 2 hours. Remove any fat from top and add onions, mushrooms and salt pork. Adjust seasonings. Remove bouquet garni. Freeze. To serve, defrost and cook at 325° for 30 to 45 minutes.

BARLEY PILAF
(8 servings)

Sauté

½ pound sliced mushrooms

in

¼ pound hot butter

Remove mushrooms. Add to pan and cook until wilted

2 chopped onions

Add

1¾ cups pearl barley   1 teaspoon salt

Stir constantly until barley is dark golden brown. Add mushrooms and

1¾ cups chicken broth

Cover and bake 30 minutes at 350°. Add another

1¾ cups chicken broth

Taste for seasoning. Bake 30 minutes more. Add stock if barley becomes dry. Cook an additional 15 minutes. Freeze. To serve, defrost and bake in 350° oven for 30 minutes.

PINEAPPLE CRUMB TORTE
(8 servings)

Cream until frothy

½ cup butter   1½ cups confectioners' sugar

Add and beat again

2 eggs

Butter an 8 x 8-inch pan. Spread with

¼ cup graham-cracker crumbs

Cover with above mixture. Drain and add

1 #2 can crushed pineapple

Cover with

1 cup heavy cream, whipped

Top with

¼ cup graham-cracker crumbs

Freeze. To serve, defrost in refrigerator.

SUNDAY BRUNCH

MELON
CINNAMON HORNS (p. 114)
* SPRING OMELETTE
BEVERAGE

A Spring Omelette is made by spreading an omelette with slightly warmed cottage cheese, broiled tomato slices and bacon strips.

SUNDAY DINNER

* VICHYSSOISE
* ROAST DUCK WITH FRUIT STUFFING
* ASPARAGUS CASSEROLE
* SWEET POTATO SURPRISE
BLUEBERRY PIE (p. 128)
COFFEE, TEA

VICHYSSOISE
(6 to 8 servings)

Clean the white part of

6 large leeks

Cut them into small enough dice to make 1½ cups. Dice

½ cup onion

Melt in heavy soup kettle

1 tablespoon butter

Add leeks and onion, cover and cook slowly, stirring occasionally for a few minutes, until soft but not brown. Peel and dice

3¼ cups potatoes

To the kettle add the

Potatoes
3 cups hot water   2 teaspoons salt

Cook slowly for 30 to 40 minutes, or until potatoes are very soft. Strain the soup or put in blender. Return to kettle and add

1 cup light cream   1 cup hot milk

Bring to boil, stirring occasionally to prevent scorching. Puree again; cool. Freeze. To serve, defrost and add

1 cup heavy cream

Mix well. Serve thoroughly chilled. Garnish with

Sprinkling of freshly chopped chives

ROAST DUCK WITH FRUIT STUFFING
(8 servings)

Defrost ducks and stuff the night before roasting. Rub

2 5-pound ducks

with

Garlic

Season cavities with

Salt

Stuff with following dressing. Truss the duck and refrigerate. To serve, roast in uncovered pan on rack at 325° for 30 minutes to the pound. If duck is very fat, prick the breast and let some fat run out. Baste occasionally.

FRUIT STUFFING
(7 cups)

Drain into saucepan

1 1-pound can sliced apples

Add to liquid to make 1 cup

Water

Heat to boiling. Stir in until melted

½ cup butter

Add and mix lightly

1 package ready-mix bread stuffing   1 cup chopped peanuts
Apples from can   ½ cup seedless raisins

Freeze. Defrost and stuff ducks.

ASPARAGUS CASSEROLE
(8 servings)

Combine

1½ cups sour cream   ⅛ teaspoon pepper
1 small onion, grated   ⅓ teaspoon dry mustard
¾ teaspoon salt   1 clove garlic, minced

Spoon over

   3 pounds cooked asparagus

in 1½-quart casserole. Mix together and sprinkle over casserole

   3 tablespoons butter   1 cup bread crumbs

Freeze. To serve, defrost and bake at 375° for 20 minutes.

SWEET POTATO SURPRISE
(14 balls)

A delightful new twist

Mix together thoroughly

8 large sweet potatoes, cooked and mashed	1 teaspoon grated orange rind
2 eggs	1 teaspoon brown sugar
1 tablespoon butter	½ teaspoon vanilla

Form into large balls. Place in center of each ball

   1 large marshmallow

and cover it well with mashed-potato mixture. Roll each ball in

   Cornflake crumbs

Freeze. When ready to serve, defrost and bake at 400° in buttered baking dish for 10 minutes.

Menus, Additional Suggestions

FRIDAY DINNERS

1. Clams Normande (p. 142)
   Lasagna (p. 94)
   Parmesan Rolls (p. 186)
   Green Salad
   Tortoni (p. 209)

2. Tipsy Cheese Spread (p. 150)
   Oysters in Cream (p. 181)
   Cranberry Nut Rolls (p. 165)
   Grapefruit Avocado Freeze
    (p. 179)
   Potato Puffs Parmesan (p. 57)
   Sherbet with Liqueur (p. 201)

SATURDAY LUNCHES

1. Quiche Lorraine (p. 184)   2. Hamburg Surprise (p. 33)
   Red-and-White Mold (p. 171)   Rolls
   Oatmeal Toll House Cookies   Lettuce and Tomato
      (p. 118)   Ice Cream

SATURDAY DINNERS

1. Sausage Balls in Pastry   2. Pastry Snails (p. 100)
      (p. 147)   Mushroom Soup (p. 154)
   Chicken Amandine (p. 164)   Veal Parmesan (p. 95)
   Boulghour Pilaf (p. 224)   Peas Suprême (p. 57)
   Baked Asparagus (p. 53)   Croissants (p. 114)
   Pink-and-White Cake (p. 204)   Hot Soufflé (p. 206)

SUNDAY DINNERS

1. Cheddar Cheese Soup (p. 45)   2. Chicken in Lemon Cream
   Rock Lobster Tails (p. 69)   (p. 156)
   French Fried Onions   Carrot Cake (p. 170)
      and Green Beans (p. 55)   Green Salad
   Orange Rolls (p. 224)   Honeybuns (p. 214)
   Strawberry-Rhubarb Pie   Orange Angel (p. 203)
      (p. 132)

Recipes by Category

HOT HORS D'OEUVRES

Broiled Jumbo Shrimp, 139
Chafing-Dish Meatballs and Franks, 140
Cheese Boereg, 64
Cheese Cigarettes, 140
Cheese Lobster Rolls, 141
Cheese Savories, 142
Chicken in Crêpes, 89
Clams Normande, 142
Cocktail Medallions, 143
Cream Cheese and Ham Filled Cream Puffs, 98
Cream Cheese and Roquefort filled Cream Puffs, 98
Crêpes filled with Crabmeat, 91
Franks 'n' Kraut, 143
Franks in Sour Cream, 144
Little Rock Canapés, 144
Olive Cheese Balls, 145
Pastry Snails, 100
Potato Stix Parmesan, 57
Quiche Lorraine, Miniature, 145
Rolled Pancake Bites, 146
Rumaki Balls, 146
Saté, 147
Sausage Balls in Pastry Blankets, 147
Shelby's Cheese Sticks, 104
Smithfield Ham in Biscuits, 148
Stuffed Mushroom Caps, 148
Tempura, 69

COLD HORS D'OEUVRES AND FILLINGS

Almond Olive, 191
Avocado, 191
Bleu-Crab Dunk, 149
Butter Spreads, 192
Cheddar Roquefort Roll, 149
Chicken-Bacon, 192
Cognac-Cheese, 192

Cauliflower with Black Olives, 54
Corn Pudding, 54
Eggplant, 40
French Fried Onions and Green Beans, 55
Green Beans Chili, 55
Limas in Cream, 56
Party Squash, 56
Peas Suprême, 57
Spinach Balls, 58
Walnut Broccoli, 58

STARCHES

Baked Potatoes, 75
Barley Pilaf, 227
Boulghour Pilaf, 224
Cheesey Baked Potatoes, 165
Double Dream Potatoes, 54
Gnocchi alla Romana, 168
Green Noodles, 221
Individual Potato Pudding, 31
Mushroom Pilaf, 180
Orange Rice Ring, 155
Potato Puffs Parmesan, 57
Potato Stix, Parmesan, 57
Sweet Potato Surprise, 231

RELISHES AND SIDE DISHES

Applesauce, 126
Applesauce with Cranberries, 127
Cinnamon apple rings, 127
Cranberry Orange Relish, 94
Cranberry Sauce, 129
Frozen Horseradish Relish, 30
Peach Chutney, 131
Stewed Fruits, 132

SALADS

Cheese Fruit Freeze, 213
Frozen Waldorf Salad, 182
Grapefruit Avocado Freeze, 179
Green Pea Salad, 56
Red-and-White Mold, 171
Salad and Cheese Suggestions, 160
Strawberry Cottage Cheese Mold, 217

BREADS

Applesauce Bread Marlowe, 109
Brioches, 110
Caraway Cheese Bread, 41

Sour Cream Coffee Cake, 120
Toffee Crunch Cake, 214
Tydings Torte, 67
Viennese Chocolate Torte, 163

SMALL CAKES AND PASTRIES

Baklava, 66
Black Bottom Cupcakes, 195
Cream Puffs and Puff Pastry filled with Whipped Cream, 105
Danish Puff, 219
Florentines, 117
Miniature Fruit Torte, 130
Pecan Tartes, 197
Puff Pastry Turnovers, 105
Yeast Dough with Cheese Filling, 122
Yeast Dough with Pecan Filling, 122

COOKIES

Apricot Crescents, 193
Butterscotch Bars, 111
Chinese Walnut Cookies, 195
Cinnamon Horns, 114
Oatmeal Toll House Cookies, 118
Orange Balls, 119
Rolled Cookies, 198
Schnecken, 198
Toffee Squares, 121

PIES

Apple Pie, 125
Blueberry Pie, 128
French Apple Pie, 127
Strawberry Rhubarb Pie, 132

DESSERTS

Applesauce, 126
Belgian Waffles, 59
Crêpes Fourrées, 92
Crêpes Suzette, 92
Frozen Fruits Chantilly, 60
Frozen Fruits and Liqueur, 60
Frozen Strawberries Romanoff, 60
Mango Sauce, 131
Mousse à la Maison Blanche, 160
Mousse au Chocolat, 168
Plum Pudding, 119
Stewed Fruits, 132

Index